A Guide to

Canadian

Architectural

Styles

A Guide to

Canadian Architectural Styles

Leslie Maitland, Jacqueline Hucker and Shannon Ricketts

broadview press

Canadian Cataloguing in Publication Data:

Maitland, Leslie
  A guide to Canadian architectural styles
  ISBN 1-55111-004-0 (bound), ISBN 1-55111-002-4 (pbk.)

1. Architecture - Canada. I.Ricketts, Shannon.
II. Hucker, Jacqueline. III. Title.

NA740.M35 1992   720' .971   C92-094867-7

Broadview Press

In Canada: Post Office Box 1243,Peterborough, Ontario, K9J 7H5

In the United States: 269 Portage Road, Lewiston, NY, 14092, USA

In the UK: c/o Drake Marketing Services, Market Place, Deddington, Oxfordshire, OX15 OSF

Table of Contents

Foreword   7

Building in the Seventeenth and Eighteenth Centuries   9

The Seventeenth Century   9

The Eighteenth Century   12

The Quebec Style   15

The Palladian Style   21

The Nineteenth Century   31

The Neoclassical Style   35

The Gothic Revival Styles   43

    The Romantic Gothic Revival Style   43

    The Ecclesiological Gothic Revival   51

The Italianate Style   58

The Second Empire Style   64

French Gothic Revival   72

The High Victorian Gothic
Revival Style   77

The Romanesque Revival Style 84

The Château Style 93

The Queen Anne Revival Style 98

The Twentieth Century 107

The Beaux-Arts Style 111

The Edwardian Classical Style 119

The Chicago Style 124

The Modern Classical Style 132

The Art Deco Style 139

The Moderne Style 148

The Twentieth Century Revival Styles 152

    The Georgian Revival Style 152

    The Tudor Revival Style 156

    The Spanish Colonial Revival Style 158

    The Quebec Revival Style 161

The Arts and Crafts Movement 164

The Modern Gothic Style 166

The Prairie Style 172

The International Style 178

The Brutalist Style 185

The Expressionist Style 192

The Post-Modern Style 198

Glossary 205

Suggested Reading 211

Foreword

Wherever you are while you are reading these words, look up from this book for a moment. Very likely you are in or near a building of some kind. Are you aware that you can read that structure as clearly as you can read these words? Materials, function, location, style: all of these things have a story to tell about the people who put up the buildings.

This book offers you an introduction to one of the many languages of architecture: style. Why does style matter? More precisely, why do we feel a need to embellish our lives beyond the basic necessity of shelter? Clearly, there is a profound cultural need to express who and what we are, where we come from, and what we aspire to, through images of beauty, power, and grace. We call this style.

But these broad, philosophical questions are best addressed elsewhere; here we will focus on the generalities of architectural style in Canada. We will describe each style in turn, examining its origins, uses, manifestations, and evolution in Canada. We will mention briefly the ways in which function, materials, location, ethnicity, and other factors affect architectural style. Only the broadest categories of style are used here; discussion of stylistic nuances has its place in more academic works. Limitations of space prevent us from reproducing every significant building of each style; this work is a sampling, not a catalogue. Some parts of the country have more buildings by virtue of their population size and years of settlement, but we have attempted to provide a regional balance.

Take this book along with you on your excursions through cities, towns, and the countryside, and have fun matching up the buildings you see with the ones in the book. Don't be surprised if some buildings do not fit into any one category, while others seem to fit into several. Buildings are not like species of wildflowers, in which the number of variables is finite. In the hands of an imaginative architect, anything is possible, and some of the best buildings are ones that break the rules.

If this book has piqued your interest in the built environment, it has served its principal purpose. It can be a doorway, if you like, into a greater concern for that environment. Buildings — old and new, alone or in groups, in cities or the country — are all subject to change, and often not for the better. If you are interested, you can find out more about architecture at your public library, or you can join local, provincial, and national organizations that will help you voice your opinion on our built environment — your environment, your heritage.

For their assistance with this project, we thank Ann Bowering, Wayne Duford, Gordon Fulton, Frank Haigh, Frank Korvemaker, Monique Trépanier, Helmut Schade, and Janet Wright.

Building in the Seventeenth and Eighteenth Centuries

The Seventeenth Century

Wood, stone, weather, fire, and the human hand: all architecture is the composite of its materials, its place and time, and the tastes and needs of the people who built it. Before we discuss architectural styles, let us briefly overview some of the forces that shaped them. Long before the Europeans arrived in North America, building traditions of several thousand years' duration were already in place. The longhouse of the Eastern Woodland Indian, the tipi of the western Plains Indian, the longhouse of the coastal Indian, and the igloos of the Inuit were all beautifully adapted to the harsh climate and the materials that were ready to hand. Ideally suited to the habits of hunters and gatherers, these structures were meant to be abandoned or transported when these nomadic peoples moved on.

The Europeans paid little attention to the impermanent architecture of the native peoples. The French who settled in the bays and inlets of the Atlantic coastline and along the shores of the St. Lawrence River established small but durable colonies. Their buildings were a response to the climate, the available materials, and inherited architectural traditions. Of their very earliest shelters nothing remains; from accounts and drawings we learn that the earliest colonists built shelters that were crudely fashioned of poles stuck in the ground, roofed over with other bent poles and bark, constructed very much as the Eastern Woodland Indians built their longhouses. Such techniques were used for some years for mission buildings erected inland, but in Quebec itself these lean-tos were quickly abandoned in favour of more comfortable and secure works. The first generation of permanent buildings was similar to the late medieval work of northern France, to which the colonists were accustomed. Again, little of this seventeenth-century building survives intact, but we can reconstruct its appearance from descriptions and illustrations. It was a modest, unassuming architecture, for throughout most of this century New France was thinly populated, under constant threat of attack from enemy Indians and the English, operating solely as an outpost of the fishery and the fur trade until the colony came under official protection of the French Crown in 1664.

The earliest permanent buildings were timber frame, the wood used well but sparingly in the European manner. These buildings were constructed of squared timbers set upright at intervals on a sill, with the intervening spaces filled with fieldstone or a mixture of mud and stone. This technique was replaced by the mid-seventeenth century, by all-wood construction, called *pièces-sur-pièces* — (literally, piece on piece). Between the vertical timbers, shorter horizontal wooden members were slotted into place. Usually roofs were covered with wooden planks or shingles. The walls were often covered with horizontal planks as well or packed with mud to keep the wind out. Openings were few, evenly spaced, and often covered with glazed paper, as glass was scarce and expensive. Such buildings were better insulated than those with stone infill; they withstood weather, settling, and shrinkage better; and they could be built by few labourers.

In the early part of the seventeenth century, roof frames tended to be massive constructions of timber. As time passed and the colonists came to know the variety of woods they were working with, the roof frames became lighter and thinner. The characteristic roof flare of Quebec architecture — called a bellcast — was brought over from northern France. The rafter sits directly on the wall plate, so that its butt end is flush with the exterior wall. To shed water from the surface of the building, a triangular piece is attached out from the rafter. Once this is shingled over, a graceful curve is created. The *canadiens* took this form of building with them wherever they went. Some of the best surviving examples are to be found at fur trade sites in western Canada.

Stone construction appeared in the seventeenth century, at first reserved for a few more permanent structures, such as churches and seminaries, that were built in towns and villages. These more ambitious buildings bore witness to the settlers' intentions to stake their claim in the New World. Often more sophisticated stylistically than most buildings in New France, they were designed in a provincial interpretation of the classicism fashionable in France at the time. They were symmetrical, their rubble walls neatly plastered over, often having massive mansard roofs and classical details such as pediments and classical mouldings.

The Eighteenth Century

The fortunes of New France changed dramatically in the eighteenth century. Her colonies grew considerably; with expanded settlement and increased prosperity, construction increased in quantity and quality. And with this development came some of the attendant problems of greater urban density, especially fire. Often the early chimneys of the seventeenth century were no more than sticks plastered over with mud, and the fires that these unsafe chimneys caused were frequent and devastating. Montreal and Quebec City were burned to the ground on several occasions. By the eighteenth century, civic codes prohibited wooden buildings in urban areas, and so buildings were constructed of rubble fieldstone, plastered over with whitewash or stucco to protect the joints from the weather. Even so, masonry buildings were at risk. Fires started in the chimneys and spread via the timberwork of the roofs throughout the town. New laws required that chimneys be of masonry, freestanding from any wooden members. Mansard roofs were forbidden for the excess of timber that they contained. End walls had to rise well above the roof to act as a fire break. Cedar shingles were forbidden (although many ignored the law on this point), and coverings of slate and tin appeared. Wooden window frames and door surrounds disappeared in favour of cut-stone trim.

Social and political changes also made their impression upon the architecture of New France. In 1664 New France was made a Crown colony, and with its new status came a civil governor, an administrative class, and a contingent of officers and men of the French army. These changes affected the development of the colony well into the next century. The army brought engineers trained in architectural design, capable of satisfying the more refined tastes of the administrative class. Books on classical architecture were now available in the colony as well. Several large and prestigious structures appeared, especially in Quebec City, such as the Jesuit seminary, an expanded cathedral, and the Château St. Louis, among others. Stylistically these were a provincial version of French classicism, with symmetrical façades, classical mouldings such as stringcourses, corner quoins, and oculus windows in gable ends. Like major structures built in France at this time, these larger institutional buildings were erected around a central courtyard. Although the exteriors were relatively plain, certain interiors were wonderfully elegant examples of classical French woodcarving and plasterwork.

Other forces shaped the appearance of buildings in the eighteenth century. Since Quebec and Montreal were fortified cities at this time, land within the walls was always at a premium. For this reason, buildings were erected right up to the street and rose several storeys. As the population of Quebec expanded, so did the urban centres, extending far beyond their protective walls. And, as the colony became more prosperous, more buildings were erected in stone. Wood still predominated in rural construction.

Quebec architecture did not change greatly after the British captured Quebec in 1759. The architects and engineers of the French administration departed for France, leaving Quebec artisans to design on their own. Naturally, they worked in the manner to which they were accustomed. Until about 1790, the British colony in Quebec was small and did not include any architects, and in any case, with little labour or money available for new construction, most efforts were directed at repairing the buildings damaged by the bombardment. The British administration perpetuated the eminently sensible building codes set down by the French government before them. Assured of stable conditions, Quebec builders continued the building traditions that they knew so well.

A different building tradition developed in Atlantic Canada, beginning in the mid-eighteenth century with the arrival of English-speaking settlers. These came from New England as well as from England, Scotland, and Ireland. The New Englanders brought their well-practised woodworking skills, and built houses, churches, meeting houses, and public buildings in wood frame, covered with narrow clapboards. The ranks of the first wave of New Englanders were augmented after the American War of Independence when many thousands of Loyalists relocated in Canada, particularly in Upper Canada, Nova Scotia, and the newly created colony of New Brunswick. Their arrival bolstered the ranks of those used to the woodworking tradition.

Some of the immigrants from Great Britain, especially the Scots, brought refined masonry techniques with them and adapted their skills to the excellent local building stones. Masonry was a more costly building technique, generally reserved for public buildings and churches of considerable size and for military construction. Brick construction was still rare, restricted to those places where brick clay was ready to hand, such as southwestern Ontario.

As for the architectural style in which these people worked, both the immigrants from the former American colonies and those coming from Great Britain shared a common taste for classical design. As we shall see in subsequent chapters, the first great classical styles in Canada were primarily British in origin, and they shaped English and French design alike.

The Quebec Style

Quebec architecture is as much a tradition as it is a style, one that persisted for generations (and survives in a modern interpretation today), maintaining its distinctness while from time to time assimilating new influences. The examples that you will find in Quebec, eastern Ontario, parts of the Maritimes, and at certain sites in western Canada date mostly from the late eighteenth and early nineteenth centuries.

Buildings in the Quebec tradition are steep-roofed structures with thick walls and fairly plain façades. The openings are few and widely spaced, and ornamentation, if any, is usually limited to the mouldings around the door. One of the most characteristic features of Quebec building is the casement window. Older casement windows dating from the seventeenth and eighteenth centuries have as many as twelve panes to a side, while eight- and six-pane windows appear in the later nineteenth century when larger sheets of glass became available. A striking feature of these buildings is the very steep roof, occupying as much as one quarter to one third of the elevation. In the seventeenth century these roofs are often hip, but later, gable roofs take over. Dormers stud their slopes, which end at the eaves in a characteristic bellcast curve. Buildings of the seventeenth and early eighteenth centuries showed no particular concern for symmetry, but in the late eighteenth and early nineteenth centuries façades become symmetrical under the growing influence of classicism. Before the twentieth century, Quebecers often preferred to build close to the front of the lot lines, giving their cities, towns and villages a characteristic compactness.

Domestic interior decoration is fairly simple in the seventeenth and eighteenth centuries. Mouldings are delicate and fireplace openings are relatively large in order to accommodate the great logs used for heating. Ceiling rafters are exposed, with the intermediary spaces plastered over. In the mid-nineteenth century mouldings become bolder and more complex, fireplace openings smaller and more heavily ornamented, and ceilings flat and plastered with handsome and intricate decoration.

1. Warehouse (1889), Fort St. James, British Columbia (above)

Typical wooden construction in the Quebec tradition is the *pièces-sur-pièces* method, in which short, squared timbers are used as infill between vertical posts. Quite a sizeable structure could be built using this method, and could later be enlarged with very little difficulty. Often these buildings were plastered or boarded over to reduce drafts. Some of the best surviving examples of *pièces-sur-pièces* construction are to be found in western Canada, erected there by fur traders coming from Quebec and from Scotland.

2. Du Calvet House (1770), 401 St. Paul Street, Montreal, Quebec (facing page)

The Quebec townhouse began to take on its present form during the eighteenth century. From one to four and even more storeys in height, this building is usually constructed of fieldstone that was originally plastered over to protect the mortar from the weather. Door and window trims are of cut stone. In the nineteenth century, cut-stone façades begin to appear, but typically just the street façade was given such expensive treatment. Crowning the structure is a steep gable roof set between high end walls that serve as fire breaks. Often the roof is covered with metal (originally tin) and has one or two rows of dormers. This type of townhouse continued throughout the nineteenth century dressed up in the various revival styles. The best places to see this urban architecture are Quebec City and Old Montreal.

3. Manoir Mauvide-Genest (1734), 783 Avenue Royale, Saint Jean, Quebec (above)
One of the delights of the Quebec countryside is the *maison traditionnelle*. These houses are long
wood or stone structures, with their entrances usually somewhere near the middle of the long side,
capped overall by a massive roof. In the seventeenth and eighteenth centuries this roof is usually a
hip, but in the nineteenth century the gable roof gradually takes over. Here we find the characteristic bellcast flare of the roof. In the nineteenth century this flare was elongated to create a covered porch along one side. Like their city cousins, these houses have casement windows and dormers. And, like the city townhouses, the rural *maison traditionnelle* weathered the battle of the styles
quite nicely, absorbing Neoclassical, Italianate, and other decorative fashions in turn.

**4. Notre-Dame-des-Victoires (1688 and subsequent dates), 9–11 Place Royale, Quebec, Quebec
(Claude Baillif and others, architects) (facing page)**   The Quebec style churches that exist today
are virtually all late eighteenth and early nineteenth century buildings; earlier ones have been demolished or modified beyond recognition. They are rectangular structures with the main entrance on the
short gable end. Some churches have lateral transepts, and some have round or squared apses. The
older churches are entirely of fieldstone that was originally plastered, with cut stone reserved for
trim around the openings. Early in the nineteenth century cut stone came into use for the entire
main façade, and later in the century we find it used for all façades. Usually the bell tower, or *clocher*
is placed over the main façade at the apex of the roof.

5. Seminaire (1675–1875); 1, côte de la Fabrique, Quebec City, Quebec (various architects) (above)
The large institutional buildings of New France followed the European models for such buildings. They were several storeys in height, with the wings arranged around central courtyards. Most of these buildings were constructed of fieldstone plastered over, with cut stone reserved for door and window openings and for decorative features. Decoration was scant, consisting of a few classical motifs, such as columns and a pediment around the door. These large institutions were usually situated on sizeable chunks of property, often walled, with attractive formal gardens.

The Palladian Style

Palladianism was the first of the great architectural styles brought to Canada by the British. Introduced in the late eighteenth century, the style thrived through the first three decades of the nineteenth century. In this style we find a symmetrical and neatly ordered façade and interior. Usually there is a prominent basement storey of rusticated stone, and above that a high main storey with smooth walls. The windows on the main level are tall, with handsomely moulded surrounds. Where a third storey exists, it is shorter, with smaller and more plainly treated windows. The roof is usually a gable or a truncated hip, set at a low pitch. On larger structures such as public buildings there is often a projecting frontispiece. Smaller structures are not so grand, but they have a handsomely designed front door, with sidelights and a transom or pediment over the door. Sometimes there is a venetian window in the centre of the upper storey, or some other decorative window treatment. Grander structures have lateral wings to either side of the main block of the building. The corners of the building are often finished off with pilasters or quoins, and a cornice runs around the building at the roofline. Stone was preferred for public buildings and for certain large and grand private homes. The style was also interpreted in wood and, less commonly, in brick. Floor plans were usually symmetrical, with rooms opening off a centre hall. Interior decoration consists of delicate mouldings of classical origin around doors and windows.

This style appeared in Canada some years after its peak of popularity in Great Britain in the early eighteenth century. Named for sixteenth-century Italian architect Andrea Palladio (1508–80), the style stressed a sober classicism of symmetry and hierarchy best expressed by certain country houses. Also influential were the London churches of architect James Gibbs, which distantly recalled the temples of ancient Rome with their pediments in the gable end and colonnades or applied orders. This dignified and relatively inexpensive design for church architecture became a formula for church design imitated throughout the British Empire.

The style came to Canada by various means. Copies of the famous architectural treatises of the era were available in a limited way, but it was the builders' manuals — like our how-to books of today — that brought classical design into the hands of craftsmen and builders. British army engineers occasionally erected buildings (as well as fortifications), and these structures were built in a conservatively Palladian style. The immigrants who arrived from Great Britain in the years 1750–1830 and the Loyalists who arrived from the United States after 1783 both brought with them a memory of a conservatively classical architecture. Quebec architects were much influenced by Palladianism and adapted it to their existing tastes and traditions, such as casement windows and steep roofs.

Although Palladianism was no longer a mainstream architectural style in Canada after the 1830s, certain of its features influenced vernacular building throughout the rest of the century. It was an approach to small house design that was persistently satisfying, generation after generation: look for symmetrical façades with centre doors, often having some decoration such as sidelights or a pediment over the door.

6. Holy Trinity Anglican Cathedral (1800–1804), 31 Desjardins, Quebec City, Quebec (Captain Hall and Major Robe, architects) (facing page)　The Palladian churches built in Canada are modelled upon those of London architect James Gibbs. The entrance is on the gable end under a pediment. The steeple sits at the front of the church on the peak of the roof, and it is staged in squares and polygons of classical inspiration. Often there are classical columns or pilasters around the door, or across the façade as here. Round-headed or rectangular windows are set at regular intervals along the sides of these buildings, while a venetian or other decorative window graces the altar end. Note the prominent blocks called quoins around the doors.

7. Former Government House (1826–28), 20 Woodstock Road, Fredericton, New Brunswick (J.E. Woolford, architect) (above)

The public buildings of the colonies were modelled on the great country houses of Britain. In our earliest assembly buildings, governors' mansions, court houses, and jails, the Palladian formula is

often repeated. They are symmetrical with a prominent rusticated basement storey. On top of this is a high main storey with tall, decorated windows, and above this is a smaller attic storey with simpler window surrounds. Often there is a grand portico in the centre. Classical orders and mouldings are employed inside and out.

8. Admiralty House (ca. 1815–19), Gottingen Street, Halifax, Nova Scotia (above)
The houses of this era were designed like the public buildings, although more modest in size. These houses are two- to two-and-a-half storeys high, with a gable or truncated hip roof, five bays wide and with a centre door. Our attention is focused around the door, where there may be sidelights or an applied order, or a porch as we see here. Grander houses sometimes have a rusticated base storey, corner quoins, or lateral wings.

9. 58 St. Louis (1830), Quebec City, Quebec (facing page)
Townhouses use a modified version of the house formula. Usually they are three bays wide instead of five, and with the door to one side instead of in the middle. The formula of base, main, and attic storey is sometimes suggested by differing window sizes, the attic windows being the smallest. Note the classical columns and delicate pediment that frame the door.

10. St. Mary's Anglican Church (1790), Auburn, Nova Scotia (W. Matthews, builder) (facing page)
Small buildings such as this fine church illustrate how well Palladianism could be scaled down and adapted to modestly sized buildings. The placement of the tower and spire before the pediment imitates certain English churches. The pilasters around the door, with a surmounting pediment, and the pediment inscribed in the gable end are all relatively easy techniques for wood construction, yet they are executed here with an eye for delicacy. Such a formula was widely used in small church design.

11. The Mill Restaurant (1842), 555 Ottawa River Parkway, Ottawa, Ontario (above)
Classicism survives in vernacular building for very nearly the rest of the century, albeit in a highly simplified form. The symmetry, horizontal proportions, and evenly spaced openings provide a useful shell for many functions while giving an air of dignity to even the most utilitarian of structures, such as this former mill.

The Nineteenth Century

The nineteenth century gave us our greatest number and variety of surviving historic structures. Numerous factors shaped the architecture of this dynamic period in our history. Patterns of settlement, the beginnings of industrialization and urbanization, the maturation of the architectural profession, social changes, and of course, new ideas in design all contributed to the emergence of an array of architectural styles.

A convenient starting point for nineteenth-century architecture is after the Napoleonic Wars, when British North America experienced an unprecedented increase in European immigration. At first most of the newcomers settled in the towns and cities of Atlantic Canada, Quebec, and Ontario. As the century advanced, the population spread westward to Manitoba, the North-west Territory (Saskatchewan and Alberta), and British Columbia. While much of this settlement was originally agricultural, by the end of the century the population had become predominantly urban.

Industrial development affected architecture in two ways. As the century progressed, more and more facets of the building industry became industrialized: component parts such as mouldings and metalwork could be mass produced and the lumber industry began to standardize. Improved manufacturing techniques transformed the production of almost all materials used in construction, such as glass, iron and steel structural members, and brick. Industrialization in turn required new categories of buildings to serve the needs of an expanding urban population: water filtration plants, fire halls, exhibition halls, and factories, among others. At the same time, existing building types such as hospitals and schools were dramatically transformed. Confederation in 1867 provided the impetus to create public buildings. In particular, the distinctive and highly visible public structures favoured by the new federal government soon enriched the emerging urban fabric. The result of these interrelated and complex developments was a greatly enlarged building stock whose appearance was quite different from anything previously seen.

After centuries of dealing with the threats of fire and disease, society now demanded buildings and cities that were healthy and safe. Improved heating and ventilating systems were invented, water supply and sewage removal were improved, and the advent of gas and then electricity made homes and cities brighter and safer. The introduction of the bicycle, horse-drawn trams, and, finally, electric streetcars made it possible for people to move away from the noise and dirt of commercial and industrial centres into cleaner, quieter residential communities. It was towards the end of this period also that reformers persuaded civic governments to create healthier living spaces through the establishment of urban parks.

Three themes stand out in the evolution of architectural style in the nineteenth century: the philosophy of the picturesque, historicism, and the survival of traditional forms.

Among the early nineteenth-century immigrants were the first professional architects to practise in Canada. Trained in the European architectural tradition, they introduced the new picturesque concepts, which were then challenging the well-established rules of design. Since the Renaissance, architectural beauty had been understood to inhere in the subtle harmonious shapes, balances, and proportions of classical architecture. The classical concept of perfection crumbled under the weight of the romantic movement, which had gained momentum in the second half of the eighteenth century. Architecture now came to be understood and appreciated in terms of its relationship to nature. Good architecture enhanced its natural surroundings and, in turn, derived its aesthetic value from nature.

The picturesque concept of architecture took hold in the 1820s and ran as a persistent undercurrent throughout the century. In the first half we see it expressed in a very subtle manner in the scenic qualities of early country villas and in certain Gothic Revival churches. By the 1840s and 1850s, however, the ideals of the picturesque had taught architects to break open the classical shell and make buildings reach out and up into the surrounding landscape or cityscape. Structures began to acquire pleasingly irregular skylines composed of prominent roofs, towers, tall chimney stacks, and dormer windows. Ground plans embraced the surrounding landscape through terraces, and verandahs. Everything was calculated to yield maximum picturesque effect.

Closely related to the philosophy of the picturesque was the revival of historical styles that could more easily express the romantic and picturesque concepts of beauty. The revival of the styles started tentatively with the Neoclassicism of the 1820s. The Italianate and the Romantic Gothic Revival followed soon after, as architects sought historical motifs that were intrinsically expressive of the purpose of the building. At this time, such historical details were added to buildings whose self-contained proportions were still fundamentally classical in spirit. After mid-century, richer and more fully developed historical styles began to appear: the Second Empire, Romanesque Revival, Château, the Queen Anne Revival, and the various Gothic Revival styles, among others. By the 1880s, architects had abandoned any pretext of historical accuracy and were reinterpreting styles to their own liking, combining elements of different architectural themes in one eclectic design. This highly creative phase is quintessentially nineteenth-century in spirit, and is often referred to as "High Victorian architecture."

The impact of historicism varied considerably within Canada, whose far-flung regions, each with its own climatic conditions and building materials, had developed strong traditions of their own. In Atlantic Canada, for example, classicism and the traditions of wood construction remained important factors. Thus, many charming vernacular versions of the high styles were developed using wood as the principal material, and manifesting the underlying persistence of classicism. In Quebec, the vigorous survival of a two-hundred-year-old building tradition, which included a distinct domestic and religious form of architecture, ensured that that province's nineteenth-century architecture possessed characteristics not found elsewhere in the country. While all of the revival styles appeared in Quebec, they were often modified in a manner that acknowledged indigenous traditions. Understandably popular were revival styles with a particularly French flavour such as the Second Empire, the Château style, and Beaux-Arts classicism. The Prairie provinces were settled later in the century, and their architecture reflected the limitations of pioneering settlement. British Columbia was a slightly older colony. Its milder climate, English traditions, and cultural connections with the American West Coast made for a distinctive and sometimes flamboyant architecture whose design and materials reflect these conditions.

Despite regional differences, nineteenth-century architecture remains easily recognizable throughout the country. This is due in part to the period's love of ornament, which was an essential ingredient of all the styles. Taking the form of applied sculpture, pattern work, colour, the play of light and shadow across the surface of the building, and contrasting textures, it enhances a great many Victorian buildings. Indeed, ornament was often seen as the essential ingredient of the design. Red, blue, and cream brick, coloured slate roofs, contrasting stones, cedar shingles, turned woodwork, terracotta panels, stained glass, cast and wrought iron, all entered into and enriched the architectural vocabulary. Interiors were similarly embellished with plasterwork, carved woodwork, sculpture, and coloured tiles and marbles. One happy result of this interest in decoration was the revival of craftsmen's arts, such as stone-carving, woodworking, and stained glass making.

Finally, thanks to advances in engineering, nineteenth-century architecture is distinctive for its new structures, such as department stores, large office buildings, drill halls, and exhibition buildings, which made their appearance in the second half of the century. Some owed their design to the properties of iron, steel, and glass, whose potential began to be exploited from mid-century onwards, enabling engineers to achieve wider spans and greater heights than ever before. In the last quarter of the century, the manufacture of large sheets of plate glass was an important innovation for commercial architecture, as was the construction of entire building façades in cast iron. The most significant engineering development, however, was the design of iron- and steel-framed buildings, whose outer walls no longer carried the weight of the structure. With the related introduction of the electric elevator, which permitted buildings to rise above five stories, the arrival of the twentieth-century skyscraper was at hand.

It was inevitable that nineteenth-century architecture would produce a reaction among a new generation of architects, engineers, and builders. By the 1890s, a disciplined classical school had emerged and Victorian architecture was on the wane. Today it forms the bulk of our architectural legacy. While it has often been a victim of unsympathetic city planning and has been forced to give way to expressways, shopping plazas, modern office buildings, and general urban sprawl, it has in more recent years enjoyed a kinder fate as Canadians have rediscovered their nineteenth-century buildings. Once considered an aberration, they are now appreciated for their human scale, their creation of pleasant urban spaces, and their satisfying image of progressive optimism and well-being.

The Neoclassical Style

The Neoclassical style first made its appearance in Canada in the early 1820s and remained popular until the 1850s. As its name suggests, it was a new kind of classicism, different in several ways from Palladianism. The symmetry of classical design persists, along with generally horizontal proportions, moderately pitched roofs, and classical details. Neoclassicism differs from Palladianism principally in its use of classical details taken directly from antique Greek and Roman prototypes, rather than from the Renaissance models. The details include Greek and Roman columns modelled directly upon the originals (especially the Ionic and the Doric orders), acanthus leaves, Greek fretwork and key designs, and earred trim. Also popular were elliptical fanlights, blind arcades, and parapets along the roofline. There was some difference in the treatment of surfaces and composition as well. Palladian architecture favoured strongly pronounced mouldings and surface textures, while Neoclassicism favoured flatter, almost linear treatments. Large Palladian buildings tended to have a prominent centre section with symmetrically placed wings; large Neoclassical buildings tended to be single, unified blocks with no wings. Additionally, one occasionally finds a Neoclassical building that is in the shape of a Greek temple; that is, it is a rectangle with a Greek Doric or Ionic colonnade either on four or three sides of the building or just on one short side, in front of the entrance. Stone is the material of preference for large public buildings, wood and brick for smaller structures.

Generally, floor plans are symmetrical, with the rooms opening from a centre hall. Neoclassical decorative details were used for interior decoration as well, including colonnettes around chimney openings, classically inspired cornices, acanthus leaves in ceiling rosettes, earred trim around doors and windows, fretwork, and key designs.

Neoclassicism, which first appeared in Europe in the second half of the eighteenth century, was a product of the romantic movement, born of a fascination with the long ago and the far away. During the eighteenth century, archaeological work began in earnest in Italy and Greece to unearth the ruins of Europe's ancient past, which until then was relatively unknown. What the archaeologists and architects found were architectural forms somewhat different from the Renaissance-inspired models to which they had been accustomed. The antique prototypes were generally simpler, bolder, less ornate. Quickly, new motifs and building types based upon the antique began to appear in new European designs and were very influential in Canada as well. The style was brought to Canada principally by the British architects and builders who emigrated in the early part of the nineteenth century, and by architectural pattern books intended for builders.

12. Colonial Building (1847-50), 78 Military Road, St. John's, Newfoundland (Patrick Kough, architect) (facing page, top)   Rapid growth in British North America during the first half of the nineteenth century meant many institutional buildings were needed, such as legislative assemblies, colleges and universities, city halls, post offices, and custom houses. Public buildings in the Neoclassical style are two to three storeys in height, often with the ground floor executed in smoothly finished masonry. The entrance is through a monumental portico, usually in the Ionic (as here), Doric, or Tuscan orders. The roof is often at a lower pitch than we see here, or in some cases even disguised by a parapet. The wall surface is smooth, with subtle mouldings around the windows, stringcourses, end pilasters, and blind arcades.

13. Rockwood Villa (1841-42), 740 King Street West, Kingston, Ontario (George Browne, architect) (facing page bottom)   Freestanding houses have a centre door, often capped by a fanlight and flanked by sidelights or pilasters. Occasionally there is also a fine front porch supported by columns. Here, there is a rather more monumental portico, with the entrance inset behind it. Stucco is not as commonly used as brick, wood, or stone. There are simple mouldings around the windows, and the roof is at a fairly shallow pitch.

14. 9 Haldimand (ca. 1830), Quebec City, Quebec (above)
Townhouses are designed in a manner similar to the freestanding houses, except that usually the door is to one side. Decoration is concentrated around the entry, where there is a pair of sidelights, and perhaps a pair of pilasters. The channelled masonry and blind arcade on the ground floor are typically Neoclassical.

15. Saint-Gregoire (1850), Nicolet, Quebec (Augustin Leblanc, architect) (facing page)
In Quebec Neoclassical church design the surface treatment is rich and complex, pointing to the influence of French Neoclassicism. This church illustrates the classic formula of the Quebec church: a pedimented front with flanking towers, five bays wide, with stringcourses and an entablature that unite the façade. The stonework is characteristically Neoclassical in its smoothness and subtlety.

16. Queen's County Court House (1854), 141 Church Street, Liverpool, Nova Scotia (William G. Hammond, architect) (above)   The Greek temple inspired Neoclassical buildings such as this one. As in its prototype, the main entrance of the Court House is through the short, gable end. A simple order of Greek Doric columns, with a prominent frieze and entablature, and a pediment inscribed in the gable, give weight and dignity to this small wooden building.

17. 5270 Morris Street (ca. 1834), Halifax, Nova Scotia (above)   Many fine vernacular buildings were built with Neoclassical details. Classical features originally intended for stone construction, such as columns and entablatures, were translated into wood and produced some very handsome results. Notice the Ionic pilasters around the door of this house.

18. Victoria and Grey Trust Building (1842), corner of William and Brock Streets, Kingston, Ontario (George Browne, architect) (above) Very few commercial buildings of the early nineteenth century have survived to this time. Those that exist are usually stone or brick, and their surfaces are articulated by simple, flat pilasters; broad, flat entablatures; stringcourses; and openings with simple mouldings or no mouldings at all. The ground floor here is a rare and very handsome arcade.

The Gothic Revival Styles

The Gothic Revival style is, because of its characteristic pointed arch, perhaps the most readily recognizable of the historical revival styles. Gothic architecture of the Middle Ages (that is, from the twelfth to the fifteenth centuries) was fundamentally very different from the classical architecture that had preceded it. While classical architecture was based upon the post and lintel system of support, Gothic architecture was based upon the structural tension created by the pointed arch and the buttress. This was an extremely sophisticated structural system, one that did not lend itself well to revival in the nineteenth century. What we tend to find instead is a revival of the pointed opening and the buttress as decorative features, as well as the other decorative motifs associated with the Gothic style. These include label mouldings over doors and windows, buttresses, pinnacles, crenellation, lancet, and rose windows. In Canada, the Gothic Revival was one of the longest lived of our revival styles: it first appeared in the 1820s and continued throughout the rest of the nineteenth century and well into the twentieth. There were so many buildings erected in the Gothic Revival, and they varied so greatly, that it is worth while taking a look at the different phases of the Gothic Revival that appeared in the nineteenth century.

The Romantic Gothic Revival Style

The first phase of the Gothic Revival was from the 1820s to the 1850s and was principally a decorative approach to the use of medieval details. By this we mean that there was no attempt to use Gothic detail with any kind of historical accuracy, nor to recreate whole buildings or the structural systems of the Gothic. The pointed arch, the label moulding, and the buttress appear on buildings that, because of their overall symmetry, horizontal proportions, and low-pitched roofs, are in fact classical in design, at heart very like the Palladian and Neoclassical buildings of the time. These historical details were furthermore taken from several of the various periods of the Middle Ages. Wood, stone, and brick were all used for these buildings. The effect was not very scientific, but it was very pretty. As for the interiors, we find Gothic Revival details such as clustered columns, pointed vaults, and even fan vaults, but again the symmetry of the floor plans suggests that classical tastes were still the guiding force behind planning and decoration.

Interest in the Gothic era first began in the mid-eighteenth century in Britain as an aspect of the romantic era. There was a revived interest in everything medieval; the history, dress, ethics, manners, customs, and, of course, the architecture. At first, medieval architectural forms were used solely for their decorativeness, and a number of country villas appeared in the style. The Romantic Gothic Revival received official support with the passage of the Church Building Act of 1818, which enabled a government commission to assist in the construction of nearly two hundred churches throughout the industrialized parts of England. These churches had the floor plans and general proportions of the classical churches of the eighteenth and early nineteenth centuries (see *Palladian Style* and *Neoclassical Style*). Yet many were given a fancy dressing of Gothic Revival detail. A second event that gave the Gothic Revival further impetus was the decision in 1835 to rebuild the recently burned Palaces of Westminster in the Gothic Revival style. As the principal public work undertaken in the first half of the nineteenth century, this project was very influential.

In Canada, the use of Gothic Revival detail in a strictly decorative manner was never entirely abandoned, even when more historically correct tastes later appeared (see *Ecclesiological Gothic Revival Style* and *High Victorian Gothic Revival Style*). These buildings have the symmetry and proportions of classicism with the details of the Gothic Revival, and as a body they constitute a readily recognizable vernacular type found throughout the country.

19. Notre Dame (1823–29), Place d'Armes, Montreal, Quebec (James O'Donnell, architect) (facing page)   It is easy to see the essentially classical spirit of this great monument in the strong horizontal lines of the stringcourses and in the overall rectilinearity of the design. Notre Dame resembles the Commissioners' Churches then being built all over England, although, ironically, Notre Dame was built for the Roman Catholic Church. The interior decoration of this building, while extremely beautiful, reflects later and very different tastes.

20. St. John's Anglican Church (1824–25), 85 Carleton Street, Saint John, New Brunswick (John Cunningham, architect) (facing page)   The Romantic Gothic Revival quickly became the architectural style for Protestant churches in Canada. In this early phase of the style, one can readily discern the classical proportions of the building and make out the shadow of a pediment in the triangulation of the gable end. The ogive arch over the main door is Moorish in origin, occasionally seen in this early phase of the style. The Gothic pointed arch applied to the façade of a basically classical building was a formula that was popular with designers of vernacular churches for the rest of the century.

21. Middlesex County Courthouse (1827–31), 399 Ridout Street North, London, Ontario (John Ewart, architect) (above)   There were few public buildings and houses erected in the Romantic Gothic Revival, since classical styles were still preferred for these types of structures. These public buildings are usually symmetrical, with flattish surfaces and low-pitched roofs. The Gothic Revival detail is limited to some label mouldings around doors and windows and some crenellation along the roofline. In general, these buildings suggest the distant influence of medieval baronial halls.

22. 152 Watson Street (ca. 1840), Saint John, New Brunswick (John Cunningham, architect) (above)
It is easy to imagine this house dressed up with a classical suit of clothes, just like the houses described in Neoclassicism. The application of Gothic Revival label mouldings around the doors and drip mouldings along the eaves gives the building a certain wedding cake quality. In houses such as this, Gothic Revival detail usually consists of nothing more than a pointed window in the gable or windows with label mouldings on an otherwise symmetrical, classically inspired design.

23. St. Andrew's Anglican Church (1845–49), Lockport, Manitoba

Many churches used the Gothic Revival only in its most basic form: the plain, pointed opening. Especially in outlying or in newly pioneered areas we find these very simple structures with pointed windows ornamenting their solid, otherwise unadorned exteriors. Such churches were built well into the twentieth century.

24. St. Paul's Anglican Church (1902), Dawson, Yukon Territories (above)
Erected nearly eighty years after the first appearance of the Gothic Revival style in Canada, this church epitomizes the durability of the style, which for many people has come to symbolize religious architecture. Notice the low, horizontal lines of the building and the sense of rectangularity, which are essentially classical in spirit.

The Ecclesiological Gothic Revival

In the 1840s there appeared a type of Gothic Revival church architecture very different from that of the earlier Romantic Gothic Revival. The fundamental classicism of the Romantic Gothic Revival is gone; Gothic Revival architecture now becomes more like the original, and we find practically authentic medieval church plans and elevations, as well as historically accurate decorative detail. When we look at an ecclesiological church, we see a building of bold and massive forms, prominent towers and buttresses, steeply pitched roofs, and deeply carved mouldings. There is a greater sophistication in the relationship between interior and exterior design, so that we can readily discern from the exterior how the interior spaces of nave, side aisles, transept, and chancel are organized. These distinct volumes give the churches an organic quality, as though they had grown over centuries the way medieval churches often did (despite the fact that the nineteenth-century churches usually were conceived of and built at one time). Stone and brick were the preferred materials for these churches, but there were also some fine structures in wood, particularly in board and batten.

Changes were made to interior design as well. To complete the sense of authenticity, there was a revival of medieval crafts, especially woodworking, metal working, stained glass, and tile. Many church interiors of this period are breathtakingly beautiful. The walls are generally plain or lightly tinted, and they act as foils to the handsome stone and wood carving. Floors are of wood or coloured tile, and an open wooden-beam ceiling covers all. Stained-glass windows, often the highlight of the interior decoration, fill the interior with coloured light.

Ecclesiology (meaning the science of church building) began in England in the 1830s. A group of Oxford University scholars set out to change certain modern practices of the Anglican Church by returning to medieval customs, especially by reviving the mysteries of the rite. Another group of scholars at Cambridge University (the Cambridge Camden Society, later the Ecclesiologists) provided guidance to architects in the creation of a suitable setting for reformed worship. They recommended abandoning the open hall so popular in the eighteenth century, in favour of the long, narrow space of the medieval church, complete with transepts, side aisles, a chancel, and an entrance through a north porch. This made for a strikingly different exterior, a long building with a massive and steep roof, whose various internal divisions created an arresting, angular and pyramidal composition. Although ecclesiology was originally intended for Anglican church architecture, it was influential in Roman Catholic and other Protestant church design as well.

The generation of architects who emigrated here from Great Britain in the 1840s and 1850s brought with them the ideas that were then raging through British architectural circles. New ideas were also imported via the periodicals and archaeological texts on medieval architecture that were newly available. Articles published in periodicals like *The Ecclesiologist* dealt with certain of the problems particular to building in Canada, such as the harsh climate and the relative scarcity of skilled labour. The authors recommended simpler, bolder shapes with less in the way of decorative sculpture, to minimize damage from frost. As a result, Canadian churches are plainer, more rugged, and more suited to the ungentle climate and landscape.

25. Christ Church Anglican Cathedral (1845–53), 100 Brunswick Street, Fredericton, New Brunswick (Frank Wills, architect) (facing page)
With the revival of medieval Anglican liturgy there also came a revival of specialized types of churches. Cathedrals were the largest and most complex structures, whose many purposes required nave, side aisles, transepts, chancel, tower, and north porch. All of these separate interior spaces are translated into visually distinct exterior volumes. Cathedrals are also sited on sizable properties, resembling the medieval close.

26. St. Paul's Presbyterian Church (1854–57), 56 James Street North, Hamilton, Ontario (William Thomas, architect) (facing page) The parish church is less elaborate than the cathedral, as there was no need for side aisles and the whole building could be smaller. Often the tower is over the main entrance rather than over the crossing, and the sculpture is altogether plainer, better suited to a more modest but still impressive structure. Chapels were simpler again, having no transepts, side aisles, or tower.

27. St. Saviour's (1870), Barkerville, British Columbia (above) A significant development of Ecclesiology was the adaptation of the Gothic Revival (essentially a masonry style) to wooden church construction. While ecclesiologists disapproved of wooden construction because of the impermanence of the material, it was the logical building material in the Canadian context. It was available everywhere, it was cheap, and nearly everyone knew how to work wood. Masonry work was slow and expensive and skilled masons were few indeed. In these wooden frame churches, clapboard or board-and-batten siding were nailed over top. This technique made for an attractive interpretation of the Gothic Revival, since it suggests the verticality so characteristic of the style.

28. St. Paul's Anglican Church (1892), 1 Church Street, Trinity, Newfoundland (Stephen C. Earle, architect) (facing page) Like the Romantic Gothic Revival, the Ecclesiological Gothic Revival survived throughout the rest of the century. The main volume of the church is surrounded by subsidiary volumes enclosing aisles, porches, and a chancel. The tower is well designed, without the feeling of flimsiness that many wooden towers have. The architect has sensibly abandoned wooden buttresses and simply used differently coloured boards to give a sense of rhythm to the walls.

29. 115 Dorset Street West (1847), Port Hope, Ontario (above) Board and batten was briefly popular for other types of structures as well, particularly houses. Here, only one pointed window and the trefoils in the gable ends suggest that the owner had a penchant for the Gothic — it was, after all, a church style considered unsuitable for houses. The board and batten, coupled with the steeply pitched roofs, deep eaves, and varied masses, makes for a picturesque house indeed.

The Italianate Style

As its name implies, the Italianate style, popular from the 1830s until the end of the century, revived the historical architecture of Italy. Two strands of the style proliferated. The first, the city palace model, was based upon urban palaces of the Italian Renaissance. These are essentially classical buildings with a rusticated base storey, a principal storey, and an attic crowned by an elaborately bracketed cornice. Principal façades are symmetrical. The classical vocabulary, which tends to be concentrated around the doors and windows, is rich and formal, incorporating attached columns or piers and arched or triangular pediments. Its sculptural qualities create a strong play of light and shade. The roof is usually a shallow hip, with deep eaves decorated with brackets. Interiors are sometimes very grand, with a two-storey central court and a dramatic staircase. They are highly decorated, either with rich stone and metal materials or, as is more usually the case, with *faux-marbre*, gilding, plaster, and paint work. The palace type was enthusiastically adopted for large city residences and public buildings, and was usually built of brick or stone.

A simplified version of the Italianate palace model was favoured for commercial architecture. Rows of three-storey, flat-roofed commercial brick buildings were enlivened with round-arched and rectangular windows decorated with hood mouldings or classical pediments and pilasters. Almost invariably, the façades were crowned with an ornate, oversized cornice. These purely decorative details were sometimes cheaply mass produced in the new industrial materials — cast iron and pressed metal. Italianate commercial buildings were an enduring type, to be found on main streets across the country right until the end of the century.

The other significant Italianate form was the villa. The Italianate villa first appeared in the 1830s and remained a very popular house design until the 1870s. At its most elaborate, the Italianate villa has a picturesque and varied design, dominated by a prominent entrance or corner tower. Shallow roofs, deeply overhanging eaves decorated with ornamental brackets, segmentally arched windows with hood mouldings, small balustraded balconies, wooden arcaded porches, verandahs, and corner quoins are all features of the style. Italianate villas were built initially for the well-to-do, but by mid-century, pared-down versions appeared. Such houses are two storeys high with square or L-shaped plans and, instead of a tower, a cupola or a belvedere crowns their low-pitched roofs. In the case of the most modest Italianate houses, cupolas are omitted; however, the distinctive low hipped-roof with deep overhanging eaves and decorative brackets is never cast aside.

The Italianate style came to Canada from England, where the palace type had first appeared in the 1820s with Sir Charles Barry's (1795–1860) designs for private clubs and public buildings. The Italianate villa appeared slightly earlier, with John Nash's (1752–1835) design for rural retreats. The popularity of the villas was due in great part to the wide circulation of architectural pattern books of the day.

30. Bellevue House (ca. 1841), 35 Centre Street, Kingston, Ontario (above)
In the 1840s a number of handsome villas were built along the shore of Lake Ontario by Kingston's more affluent citizens. Bellevue House, once the home of Sir John A. Macdonald, is believed to be one of the oldest Italianate buildings erected in Canada. At the time, its asymmetrical plan, centre tower, shallow roof, light eave fringe, and generous wooden verandah would have seemed very novel, especially in comparison with the Neoclassical villas under construction at the same time (**see** *Neoclassical Style*). Although the identity of the architect remains a mystery, Bellevue House may have been designed by George Browne, who also designed Kingston's City Hall.

31. City Hall (1856–67), 59 Carden Street, Guelph, Ontario (William Thomas, architect) (facing page, top) The self-assured appearance of Italian Renaissance architecture was perfectly attuned to the civic sensibilities of the mid-nineteenth century, influencing the design of many pre-Confederation public buildings. While the restrained monumentality of Guelph City Hall still shows the lingering influence of the Neoclassical style, the more exuberant treatment of its pedimented frontispiece, with its elaborate door surround, elegant venetian window, and ornamental balcony, is definitely Italianate. William Thomas was a Toronto architect who developed one of the most prestigious practices in the country.

32. 151 Victoria Avenue (ca. 1867), Belleville, Ontario (facing, bottom) Built more than twenty years after Bellevue House, this generously sized yet compact house, with a projecting frontispiece and a cupola instead of a tower, was typical of many Italianate houses after the mid-century. Its ornate wooden detailing (such as the paired scroll brackets along the eaves), the elaborate door surround, and the verandah across the front have the robust appearance favoured by the High Victorians.

33. Law Courts (1874–76), 171 Richmond Street, Charlottetown, Prince Edward Island (Thomas Alley, architect) (facing page)   The Italianate was a very popular style for public buildings. A simple, self-contained block, this building acquires the quiet grandeur of the Italian palazzo with the division of the storeys into elevated basement, main storey, and upper, and with the application of Italian Renaissance details, such as the voussoirs with prominent keystones over the windows.

34. The Former Coombs English Shoe Store (1860), 1883–85 Granville Street, Halifax, Nova Scotia (above)   This three-storey building with its evenly sized round-arched windows, decorated cornice, and flat roof is typical of Italianate commercial buildings erected in Canada in the 1850s and 1860s. It is also an early example of a cast-iron façade. The façade was manufactured in New York City and shipped to Halifax, where it was assembled on the site. The usefulness of cast iron in the mass production of architectural components made it a very popular building material in the second half of the nineteenth century.

The Second Empire Style

Second Empire buildings are recognizable, first and foremost, by their mansard roofs, a double pitched roof with a steep lower slope. The principal façades of large public buildings have a three-part composition, that is, a prominent centre section and flanking end pavilions. Their roofs and towers are decorated with ornately pedimented dormer windows and fanciful iron cresting. The rest of the building is often embellished with rich architectural details, such as paired, superimposed columns and pilasters, ranges of elaborately framed windows, and strongly moulded stringcourses. Yet despite their flamboyant appearance, these buildings have a noticeable grid-like organization, which imposes order and logic on an otherwise rich brew. This classical style was popular in the 1870s and 1880s and typifies the increasingly elaborate and monumental appearance of architecture towards the end of the nineteenth century.

The ostentatious appearance of the full-blown Second Empire style limited its use to a number of public buildings, banks, insurance companies, religious institutions, and some commercial properties. The mansard roof, however, provided an additional top storey and a rather grand appearance, so that a simplified version of Second Empire gained widespread popularity as a domestic style. Second Empire houses are particularly prevalent in St. John's, Newfoundland, and in Saint John, New Brunswick, where the style's popularity coincided with the rebuilding of the city centre after the 1877 fire, and in Quebec, where its French associations had particular appeal for both government and business. For nearly twenty years the Second Empire was the height of fashion in domestic architecture, and excellent Second Empire houses are found throughout the country.

The Second Empire style originated in France, when Napoleon III (1852–70) undertook a major redevelopment of Paris, transforming it into a city of grand, tree-lined boulevards and monumental buildings. The most influential of these buildings was the New Louvre (1852–57), whose style was a synthesis of French Renaissance (derived from the Italian Renaissance, which explains the similarity of many of its features with the Italianate) and classical French architecture. Perfectly reflective of nineteenth-century bourgeois taste, the Second Empire quickly became fashionable first in the United States and then in Canada.

35. Legislative Assembly (1877–87), Dufferin Avenue, Quebec City, Quebec (Eugène Taché, architect) (above) With its mansard roofs, centre and corner pavilion massing, elaborate silhouette and rich classical ornament, the Quebec Legislative Assembly Building displays all the basic components of the full-blown Second Empire style. The building, which is designed around a courtyard like the Louvre in Paris, lacks the superimposed free-standing columns that add a sculptural quality to Second Empire buildings. However, its sheer mass gives it the dominating presence that was much sought after by governments, religious orders, and large corporations alike. Taché designed an important group of Quebec buildings in the French Chateau and Second Empire styles.

36. City Market (1874–76), 47 Charlotte Street, Saint John, New Brunswick (J.T.C. McKean and G.E. Fairweather, architects) (above) The market was one of the few downtown buildings to escape a devastating fire that swept through Saint John in 1877. Typical of the Maritime versions of the style, its Second Empire features are restrained within the wall planes of the rectangular block. The brick and stone work is very fine and there is a hint of gaiety in the decorative brickwork under the eaves. Behind the façade is a rare nineteenth-century market hall whose roof is supported by handsome timber framing on cast-iron columns.

37. Langevin Block (1883–89), Wellington Street, Ottawa, Ontario (Thomas Fuller, architect) (above) Built to house an expanding civil service, this distinguished structure stands across the street from the Parliament Buildings. By the mid-1880s the Second Empire style was on the wane, soon to be supplanted by the eclecticism of the late nineteenth century. The Second Empire style is here blended with Romanesque Revival and Château style details, the former seen in the round-arched windows and the latter in the shape of the dormers. The building now houses the offices of the Prime Minister and Privy Council.

38. Custom House (1873–75), 1002 Wharf Street, Victoria, British Columbia (Department of Public Works, architects) (above) This building typifies the simplified Second Empire style propagated by the federal Department of Public Works across the country during the 1870s and 1880s. The mansard roof and the segmental voussoirs with prominent keystones and the elaborate arched cornice over the main door ornament an otherwise economical and simple building. This building inspired the construction of a number of public buildings in Victoria in the same style.

39. 30 Monkstown Road (1875), St. John's, Newfoundland (J. and J.T. Southcott, architects) (above)
St. John's possesses a wealth of charming Second Empire houses, perfectly attuned to the distinctive architecture of the island. Many, like this house, were built by the father and son partnership of J. and J.T. Southcott. At heart it is a typical Newfoundland house designed in the British classical tradition, dressed up with Second Empire embellishments in the form of a bellcast mansard roof, round-headed dormers, and two bay windows. Its intricately and delicately carved wooden ornament is a feature of Atlantic Canadian architecture, where there is a long tradition of superb woodworking.

40. 201 Charles Street (ca. 1879), Belleville, Ontario (above) This free-standing, two-storey residence is one of many comfortable and rather grand Second Empire houses built in Ontario in the last quarter of the nineteenth century. Constructed in a light-coloured brick, with a patterned slate roof, its massing, mansard roof, and turned wooden porches are typical of the style. The Victorian love of ornament is particularly well illustrated in the treatment of the roof, which supports a proliferation of dormer windows framed with jaunty surrounds, wooden cornices, rows of scroll brackets, and other embellishments.

41. 610 Buxton Street (1890–91), Indian Head, Saskatchewan. (above)
Prairie examples of the Second Empire style tend to be fairly plain; not so this elaborate stone house in Indian Head. The Second Empire was meant to be a formal, monumental style, but in the hands of an inventive builder it could be picturesque and playful in the exaggeration of its details, as in this example with its overblown mansard roof and decorative iron cresting. Notice the cinder blocks used as column capitals.

French Gothic Revival

In the fourth quarter of the nineteenth century, the Roman Catholic Church adopted for its larger churches and cathedrals a scaled-down and modified version of the medieval cathedrals of northern France. These buildings favoured a monumental design, built up within a well-ordered framework. Their organization is most clearly expressed on the principal façade, where the central entrance portal, the large rose window above, and the flanking twin-towers are arranged within the squares of a rectangular grid. The grid controls the design and scale of each element. Most buildings have a T-shaped ground plan consisting of an arcaded nave and side aisles, short transept arms, and a polygonal apse. The structural organization of the high interiors is often delineated by plaster ribs and shafts, which run from the apex of the roof down to the nave arcade. The interior decoration can be very ornate and colourful, particularly in the sanctuary where the high altar stands. The French Gothic Revival was primarily the preserve of the Roman Catholic Church, in whose eyes English medieval architecture had become too closely identified with the Anglican Church. The compact monumentality of French Gothic was more suited to urban settings, where a large proportion of the Roman Catholic population lived. Such was the influence of this style, though, that elements of French Gothic began to creep into the design of a number of High Victorian Gothic churches, including those erected by the Anglican Church.

The revival began in France in the middle of the century. Its well-known proponent was the theorist and architect Eugène-Emanuel Viollet-le-Duc (1814–1879). It was Viollet-le-Duc who drew attention to the structural logic of French medieval architecture and argued that progress towards a new non-historical style would be made when more attention was given to the structure of buildings. Influential also in the creation of this style was the completion of the cathedral of Cologne in Germany, which had remained unfinished since the Middle Ages. The work, recommenced in 1856 using the original medieval plans, inspired the construction of St. Patrick's Cathedral in New York City, which, in turn, influenced the design of a number of Catholic churches in the United States and Canada. Unlike other forms of the Gothic Revival, French Gothic was reserved exclusively for religious buildings.

42. Our Lady of the Immaculate Conception (1876–88), Norfolk Street, Guelph, Ontario (Joseph Connolly, architect) (above) Although it is not a cathedral, Our Lady of the Immaculate Conception, with its twin-towered façade, large rose windows, transepts, clerestory, polygonal apse, and radiating chapels, is the most ambitious attempt to erect a French-style cathedral on Canadian soil. Its design was directly inspired by the completion of Cologne Cathedral. Joseph Connolly acquired his knowledge of Gothic Revival architecture in Ireland. He set up practice in Canada in the 1870s and in the last quarter of the century designed an impressive number of Roman Catholic churches in Ontario.

43. St. Patrick's Roman Catholic Church (1912–14), 238 2nd Avenue East, Medicine Hat, Alberta (Manley N. Cutler, architect) (page 74) The well-ordered monumentality of this handsome church is quintessentially French Gothic. St. Patrick's is believed to be the first large church in Canada to be constructed of reinforced concrete. Its smooth monochromatic wall surfaces heralded not only the arrival of a new building material but also new aesthetic ideals, which were then replacing the High Victorian emphasis on decoration.

44. Chapel of Notre-Dame du Sacre-Coeur (1909–10), Sainte-Ursule Street, Quebec City, Quebec (François-Xavier Berlinguet, architect) (page 75) The French Gothic Revival was never particularly popular in Quebec, which had a strong tradition of classically inspired church architecture. The rather pinched exterior of this small church suggests that the architect had not come to terms with the style. However, the spirit of French Gothic is beautifully captured on the interior, which is bathed in a luminous light filtered through an encompassing ring of stained-glass windows.

45. St. Dunstan's Roman Catholic Cathedral (1897–1907; rebuilt 1913–19), 61 Great George Street, Charlottetown, Prince Edward Island (François-Xavier Berlinguet, architect, J.M. Hunter, architect of the interior decoration) (above) St. Dunstan's is a highly distinctive, French-inspired cathedral with a dramatic history. Erected between 1897 and 1907, it was severely damaged by fire in 1913. The citizens of Charlottetown conserved the surviving walls and immediately rebuilt the cathedral to its original exterior plans. The interior was completely redesigned by J.M. Hunter.

The High Victorian Gothic
Revival Style

In the 1850s, the Gothic Revival entered a more self-assured and eclectic phase, free from the restraints imposed by the archaeological tastes of Ecclesiology. The standard features of the Gothic Revival remained, especially the pointed opening, the buttress, and the lancet, rose, and trefoil windows, but the approach to composition and decoration changed. The High Victorian Gothic exhibits an underlying interest in bold geometric forms, solid wall surfaces, and — its most distinctive feature — polychromy, which is the use of contrasting coloured building materials as a form of decoration. By comparison to the Gothic Revival structures of the first half of the nineteenth century, High Victorian Gothic buildings appear much weightier, more massive, and monumental. The Gothic detail is integral to the design, rather than applied, and the materials are chosen for their decorative as well as their functional properties. Differently coloured building stones, iron cresting, woodwork painted in strong colours, coloured roofing slates, and contrasting brickwork were some of the great variety of materials used in this style.

The change in design was due in part to a growing interest in a wide range of European medieval models, particularly those of northern France, northern Italy, and, to a lesser extent, Germany. Choosing forms and details at will, architects broke away from historical models to create a new style. The rise of High Victorian Gothic in Canada fortuitously coincided with the commencement of a number of large and important building projects. The most significant of these was the construction of the federal Parliament Buildings, begun in Ottawa in 1856.

The High Victorian Gothic Revival originated in England in the late 1840s, with the writings of the theorist John Ruskin (1819–99) and the buildings of architect William Butterfield (1814-1900). Ruskin had been captivated by the medieval architecture of northern Italy and became passionately interested in promoting the decorative nature of architecture. In an influential book, *The Seven Lamps of Architecture* (1849), he developed a set of aesthetic architectural theories that formed the basis of High Victorian Gothic architecture.

46. Library of Parliament (1859–66; interior finished 1876), Parliament Hill, Ottawa, Ontario (Fuller and Jones, architects) (above) The Library forms part of the complex of government buildings on Parliament Hill. Designed in the manner of the round medieval chapter houses of Europe, its compact, geometric shape and the decorative handling of its differently coloured sandstones, copper roof, and iron cresting make it a splendid example of the High Victorian Gothic style. The library is perched above the waters of the Ottawa River where, in true nineteenth-century fashion, it exploited to the fullest the romantic nature of the site.

47. Post Office (1884–89), 50 Victoria Street East, Amherst, Nova Scotia (Thomas Fuller, architect) (above) The eclectic nature of High Victorian Gothic is evident in this federal government building. Influenced by civic buildings of northern Europe, its distinctive features are its tall gable end-wall, steep roof, and picturesque clock tower. The use of the dark rusticated sandstone and contrasting smooth stone trim around the pointed Gothic doors and windows is typical of the style's emphasis on decorative stonework. Thomas Fuller was the highly talented chief architect of the Department of Public Works. Thanks to him, a number of distinctive High Victorian public buildings were erected across the country.

48. St. James-the-Less Chapel (1860–61), Parliament Street, Toronto, Ontario (Frederick Cumber-land, architect) (facing page)   With its sturdy corner tower surmounted by a spire, a steep, over-sized roof, low walls, and prominent buttresses, St. James-the-Less introduced a sophisticated design for small parish churches, which emphasized weight and geometric shapes while still retaining the much-admired picturesque silhouette. The compact design adapted well to urban settings, and as a re-sult, churches similar to St. James-the-Less are found in towns and cities across the country.

49. Tryon United Church (1881), Tryon, Prince Edward Island (William Critchlow Harris, architect) (above)   Throughout the second half of the nineteenth century, the Atlantic provinces continued to develop their own versions of the Gothic Revival in wood. Here the broad, flat planes of the roof, the rectangular tower, soaring spire, and simple Gothic windows are juxtaposed in a deceptively sim-ple manner to give the small village church a strong, almost muscular presence. William Critchlow Harris was a highly gifted Gothic Revival architect who designed a number of wonderful churches in Prince Edward Island.

50. St. Andrew's Cathedral (1892), Blanshard Street, Victoria, British Columbia (Maurice Perrault and Albert Mesnard, architects) (facing page)   With its triple entrance portal, circular stained-glass window, and flanking façade towers, St. Andrew's exhibits the influence of French medieval architecture. However, its bold use of polychrome decoration is distinctly High Victorian Gothic, as are its deliberately mismatched towers. The architectural firm of Perrault and Mesnard hailed from Montreal and enjoyed a high reputation for its religious architecture.

51. Montreal Diocesan Theological College (1895–96), 3475 University Avenue, Montreal, Quebec (A.T. Taylor, architect) (above)   A number of colleges and schools were built in the High Victorian Gothic Revival style, although most were plainer than this example. Notice the use of materials of contrasting colours. Historical details are taken from several periods, and are chosen not for archaeological accuracy but for their suitability to the design. While this design is perhaps more Gothic than anything else, the features it adopts from other historical periods mark it with the eclecticism found in all of the late-nineteenth century styles.

The Romanesque Revival Style

The Romanesque Revival had two distinct phases, which arguably could be seen as two separate styles. The first phase, which appeared in Canada in the 1840s, looked for inspiration to the medieval architecture of the eleventh and twelfth centuries and had much in common with the Gothic Revival style. Its principal features are square towers, hipped and gabled roofs, and decorative medieval-inspired detailing, such as corbel tables under the eaves. The windows are round arched with wide voussoirs, and the buildings tend to have a heavier appearance than their Gothic Revival counterparts. The early Romanesque Revival style was used for some religious architecture and institutions. A stripped-down version became the standard repertoire for commercial and industrial architecture as well as for modest public buildings. It is characterized by a repetitive use of round-arched windows set in smooth brick walls articulated by thin pilaster strips. This functional interpretation of the style is not dissimilar to Italianate commercial architecture.

The early Romanesque Revival style appeared in the 1840s almost simultaneously in Europe and the United States, inspired in part by the eclecticism advocated in the writings of John Ruskin and in part by the architecture of German architect Karl Friedrich von Schinkel (1781–1841). One of the earliest known North American examples is the first museum building for the Smithsonian Institute in Washington, which was designed by James Renwick (1818–95) in 1846.

The second phase of the Romanesque Revival style emerged in the 1880s, under the influence of the American architect H.H. Richardson (1838–86), who reinterpreted Romanesque architecture in a highly individual manner. Richardsonian Romanesque (as the style is sometimes called) buildings are robust masonry structures with an originality that was new to nineteenth-century architecture. Characteristic features include walls of large rough-faced masonry blocks; massive, round-arched entrances incorporating short, polished columns and prominent voussoirs set flush with the wall; groups of deeply set windows; asymmetrically positioned short circular towers with conical roofs; heavy stone stringcourses; and oversized corbels. Despite their mass, these buildings tend to be compact and sculptural in appearance. They often incorporate sculpture, stained glass, and other arts and crafts detailing. The style was promoted widely in Canada by Thomas Fuller, who had worked in the United States before becoming the chief architect of the Department of Public Works. A number of post offices and custom houses were built in the style while he held office. The later Romanesque Revival style was also popular for houses in the 1880s and 1890s.

52. University College (1856), University of Toronto, Toronto, Ontario (Cumberland and Storm, architects) (above) This is one of the earliest as well as one of the best examples of the Romanesque Revival style. Its source of inspiration is English, or Norman, Romanesque architecture, exemplified by the projecting square tower, with its corner buttresses and round-arched entrance enriched with bands of stylized decoration, and by the tiers of varied round-arched windows. The design is very closely based upon the design of Oxford University Museum, built in 1855–59 by architects Deane and Woodward with the assistance of John Ruskin. The roof with its coloured slates and iron cresting is pure nineteenth century.

53. Basilica of Saint John the Baptist Roman Catholic Cathedral (begun 1845), St. John's, Newfoundland (above) A remarkable building for its time and place, Saint John the Baptist Cathedral illustrates well the features of the early Romanesque Revival as formulated by certain German architects. The architectural forms are essentially from twelfth-century Italy including the towers capped by hip roofs and the façade with two tiers of arcades.

54. Church of Saint Brigide (1878–80), 1151 Alexandre-De-Sève Street, Montreal, Quebec (Martin de Poitras and Martin, architects) (facing page) The Roman Catholic Church often preferred the more sober aspects of nineteenth-century architecture. When the Romanesque Revival style came into fashion, for instance, the Church revived the stern Romanesque of northern France for its churches and religious institutions. Saint Brigide's Church, with its prominent centre tower, round-arched openings, and corner buttresses is quite typical. Because it lacked any intricate exterior detailing, French Romanesque suited Montreal's severe winter climate, and, moreover, it looked good in limestone, the city's most common building material. As a result, there are a number of similar churches around the city. The elaborate steeple was added at a slightly later date.

55. Windsor Station (1888–89), La Gauchetière Street, Montreal, Quebec (Bruce Price, architect; additions [1900–06] by Edward Maxwell, architect, and [1909-14] Walter S. Painter, architect)
Windsor Station is one of Canada's finest examples of a Richardsonian Romanesque building. Its simple yet powerful massing and rough-faced stone work, together with the rhythmic lines of its tall wall

arcades, are important components of Richardson's bold compositions. Windsor Station was built as the head office of the Canadian Pacific Railway. The first transcontinental train left the station on June 28, 1886, and arrived in Port Moody, British Columbia, on July 4. The choice of American architect Bruce Price was indicative of the growing influence of American architecture in the 1880s.

56. 37 Madison Avenue (1888–90), Toronto, Ontario (Edward James Lennox, architect) (above)
This small house combines a tempered Richardsonian Romanesque at ground level with the lighter and more playful Queen Anne Revival above. The result is a splendid High Victorian concoction that set the tone for many residences in Toronto in the late nineteenth century.

57. Cardston Court House (1906–1908), 89 3rd Avenue, Cardston, Alberta (Alberta Department of Public Works, architects) (above)   Here we see the Romanesque Revival reduced to its basic forms, rusticated stone and wide window voussoirs. This is a very late example of the Romanesque Revival: notice the intrusion of classical mouldings in the eaves.

58. Lyon Building (1883), 2217-225 McDermot Avenue, Winnipeg, Manitoba (Blackmore and Black-stone, architects; two-storey addition [1905–1906], John H.G. Russell, architect) (above)
Built originally as a three-storey warehouse, this building derives its particular Romanesque Revival character from the large number and regular rhythm of its round-arched windows. With its ease of construction and emphasis on large windows, permitting plenty of light to enter the buildings, the Romanesque Revival was a popular choice for commercial buildings. In all other respects the building is typical of late nineteenth and early twentieth century warehouse buildings.

The Château Style

The grandest Château style buildings of the 1880s and 1890s are large structures with asymmetrical plans and irregular elevations, whose most distinctive features are the steeply pitched, copper covered roofs encrusted with dormers, gables, conical towers, tourelles, finials, and iron cresting. The walls are sometimes brick, but usually they are faced with smoothly finished cut stone. There are many windows, almost all of which are richly decorated. The dormer windows often have pediments and ornamental scrolls of classical origin, whereas the window gables may be highlighted with finials and crockets in the medieval manner. Stringcourses, corbel tables, and cross windows break up the wall surfaces. Because of its monumental size and lavish ornament, the fully fledged Château style was reserved for large hotels, government institutions, and imposing residences. However, the idea of living in a château had definite romantic appeal, and we find its most distinctive features, such as the steep, metalclad roof, conical towers, and tourelles, absorbed into the standard vocabulary of High Victorian eclecticism on numerous smaller public buildings and private residences.

The Château style, which was closely related in spirit to the High Victorian Gothic, was inspired by the imposing sixteenth-century French châteaux of the Loire Valley. These were fortified, late-medieval castles whose picturesque qualities blended well with the formal, classical architecture of the Italian Renaissance. Well suited to the urbane tastes of the French aristocracy, these châteaux were bound sooner or later to capture the imagination of nineteenth-century architects and their clients, particularly rich corporate clients like the railway companies, who made the style their own. The Château style was revived in France in the 1860s, from where it spread first to Britain and then to the United States. The first known example of a Château style building in Canada is the Grande Allée Drill Hall in Quebec City, which was built in 1887. The Château style was popularized by the extraordinarily successful Château Frontenac Hotel, also in Quebec City, which led to the style's use for numerous other railway hotels and stations across the country. The Château Laurier, in turn, influenced the design of a number of important federal government buildings in Ottawa in the 1920s and 1930s. By then the Château style had come to be seen as a distinctly Canadian style.

59. Grande Allée Drill Hall (1887), Quebec City, Quebec (E.E. Taché, architect) (above)
This drill hall was the first Canadian building to be designed in the Château style. Its choice of style reflected Quebec's cultural origins. Buildings like the drill hall have perpetuated the romantic image of Quebec as an old fortified town, an image that persists and that has helped to preserve Canada's most picturesque city.

60. Château Laurier (1908–12), Confederation Square, Ottawa, Ontario
(Ross and MacFarlane, architects) (facing page, top) This hotel was the first in a chain of Château hotels constructed by the Grand Trunk Railway (later incorporated into the Canadian National Railway). With its smooth stone façades and steeply pitched copper roof, richly ornamented with dormer windows, finials, and iron cresting, the Château Laurier was irresistible to travellers, and not long after it opened it was enlarged. Standing on the cliffs overlooking the Ottawa River, its picturesque silhouette had an equally strong effect on the federal government, which used it as a model for several of its buildings in the vicinity of Parliament Hill.

61. Angus McIntyre House (1894), 3490 Peel Street, Montreal, Quebec (Edward Maxwell, architect)
(facing page, bottom) The Angus McIntyre House nicely illustrates the romantic nature of late nineteenth century domestic architecture. The Château details are found in the conical roof of the round tower, the steep roof, and the gable windows. However, the weighty horizontal appearance of the house with its rough-faced masonry is typical of the Romanesque revival. Since this particular combination suggested Scottish baronial architecture as much as French châteaux, it had great appeal for affluent Montrealers of Scottish descent, who built a number of houses similar to this one.

62. Bessborough Hotel (1927), Saskatoon, Saskatchewan (John S. Archibald and John Schofield, architects) (above)   The Bessborough is the last in a great line of Château style railway hotels. Erected forty years after the Quebec drill hall and half a continent away, the steep roofs ornamented with dormers, towers, and tourelles, and the walls of stone and brick ornamented with bay windows suggest the enduring popularity of these highly romantic buildings with the travelling public.

63. West 10th Street (ca. 1928), Vancouver, British Columbia (facing page)
Not all Château-style buildings were grand hotels, government buildings, or residences of the rich. The Château style, round-towered entrance hall, with its conical roof and small windows, adds a playful note to this charming two-storey house and distinguishes it from its neighbours.

The Queen Anne Revival Style

The Queen Anne Revival style is the most eclectic of the nineteenth century styles, the most varied, colourful, and light-hearted. The historical details are taken principally from fifteenth-century English architecture, which was a blend of medieval and classical motifs. The medieval motifs include tudor windows, corner towers, bay and oriel windows, and some medieval carving. The classical features are columns and pilasters, pediments, sash windows, Palladian windows, and stringcourses. All of these motifs are combined on façades that are usually asymmetrical in elevation, with high, irregular rooflines punctuated with many dormers, gables, and ornamented chimney stacks. Projecting wings, porches, and balconies enliven the façade even more. As if this dizzying variety were not enough, the architects of Queen Anne Revival buildings executed these designs in virtually every material available. Red brick is the most commonly used, often combined with stone or wood trim or panels of sculpted terracotta. Wood is commonly used too, in a delightful number of ways: clapboard, and shingle, either left to weather naturally or painted a variety of brilliant colours. Despite this bewildering combination of details and surface treatments, there is an underlying discipline to Queen Anne Revival buildings. Usually, for each vertical there is a horizontal, for each busy surface a calm one. The composition is one of balance rather than symmetry.

The greatest number of Queen Anne Revival buildings are houses, although the style was also used for some hotels, hospitals, apartment buildings, and commercial properties. The interiors of these houses are usually designed around a central stair hall. This is a largish hall containing the stairs, seating, and a fireplace; often the principal rooms of the ground floor lead off from this central circulatory space. Queen Anne Revival style interiors feature luxurious appointments, including beautiful plasterwork and woodworking; a variety of window types; built-in bookshelves, buffets, and cabinets; glazed tile, and terracotta; and stained and bevelled glass.

The Queen Anne Revival came from England, where it had first appeared in the 1860s and 1870s, invented by a group of architects who catered to the upper-middle classes. They created large, comfortable, luxurious houses that were an instant success with London's merchant and artistic classes and that quickly became popular on this side of the Atlantic. American architects added their special interpretation of the Queen Anne Revival when they recreated it in wood, building large, clapboard-covered houses. The style ceased to be popular after the First World War, but certain aspects of its design, especially the free-flowing qualities of the interior spaces, influenced subsequent styles. The Queen Anne Revival style is presently enjoying some popularity among Post-Modern architects.

64. Laurentian Club (1909), 252 Metcalfe Street, Ottawa, Ontario (John W.H. Watts, architect)
(above)   The greatest number of Queen Anne Revival houses were built in Ontario, reflecting the prosperity of this province at the end of the century. These houses were, for the most part, built of red brick with contrasting trim. Note the characteristics of the style: a variety of window types such as venetian and bay; motifs that are both classical and medieval such as the shaped pediment and the tower, respectively; and a complex, many-gabled roof with prominent chimneys.

65. Hammond Residence (1899), 118 York Street, Sackville, New Brunswick (Burke and Horwood, architects) (facing page, top)   Queen Anne Revival houses in the Atlantic provinces were predominantly wood. One often finds a lively combination of clapboard and shaped shingles on the same building. Although many Queen Anne Revival wooden houses are now monochrome, they were often originally painted in rich combinations of colours. Some wooden houses were covered entirely with shingles, and these buildings are sometimes referred to as shingle style; the approach to exterior and interior design remains otherwise the same.

66. Hooper Residence, 243 Kingston Street, Victoria, British Columbia (Thomas Hooper, architect) (facing page, bottom)   A characteristic West Coast Queen Anne Revival house is the bungalow. The idea for these one-storey houses came originally from tropical climes, but it adapted quite nicely to British Columbia and to the revival styles. A verandah is an essential feature of these buildings. Wood is again a favourite medium, used in clapboard and shingle combinations. Tudor half-timbering (not seen here) was also popular in British Columbia. Note the combination of classical (columns, pediment) with late medieval motifs, and the high roofline.

67. Roslyn Court Apartments (1909), 105 Roslyn Road, Winnipeg, Manitoba (William Wallace Blair, architect) (above)   The Queen Anne Revival style offered interesting ideas to designers of apartment buildings. Instead of a tedious, beehive multiplication of units such as characterizes much of apartment building design today, there is a great deal of visual interest introduced by the variety of window types, the advancing bays and pavilions, the contrasts of red brick and pale stone trim, and the variegated roofline. Such apartments were often beautifully finished inside, with hardwood floors, panelling, plaster decorations on the ceiling, and leaded and stained glass.

68. Dundas Terrace (1889), Water Street, Charlottetown, Prince Edward Island (W.C. Harris, architect) (above) Apartment buildings were rarely constructed of wood because of the risk of fire (ironically, this building was badly damaged by fire recently). The architect has designed the building by using the same principles that guided the design of Queen Anne Revival houses: balances of vertical and horizontal lines; porches; steep roof with dormers; a variety of window sizes; and textured surfaces.

69. Roger's Chocolates (1903), 913 Government Street, Victoria, British Columbia (Hooper and Watkins, architects) (facing page)   The Queen Anne Revival was also used for commercial structures, for which its informality and festive quality made it ideal. Its eclectic approach to design allowed for great freedom of planning. Here, the bay and oriel windows were valued for their charm and for the large expanses of glass to display merchandise.

70. South Park Elementary School (1894), 508 Douglas Street, Victoria, British Columbia (W.R. Wilson, architect) (above)   The late nineteenth and early twentieth centuries saw a great movement towards comprehensive public school education, which led to the construction of school buildings all across the country. Many of these buildings were similar to the Queen Anne Revival style schools then being constructed in Great Britain. Red brick made for inexpensive, fireproof construction, and the informal approach to planning of the Queen Anne Revival gave designers considerable flexibility. Few other public buildings were built in that style, and the Tudor style quickly supplanted the Queen Anne Revival in school design.

The Twentieth Century

Of the forces that affected building in the twentieth century, some
had first appeared in the nineteenth century; others were completely
new, born of modern times and conditions. Noteworthy among the
latter were the technological changes that affected construction and
design, the increasing professionalism of architects, the establishment
of the modern corporate base for construction, and ideological developments in architecture that were formulated elsewhere and reinterpreted in the Canadian context.

The twentieth century is as remarkable, architecturally, for the size
of its buildings as it is for their styles. The increase in scale, at least
in public and commercial structures, was due in part to the widespread application of such building techniques as the structural steel
frame and the passenger elevator, which were born in the previous
century. But it was in the twentieth century that the potential of this
technology reached fruition. The manufacture and installation of
these systems were refined, and to them was added reinforced concrete, a substance that has had a remarkably liberating effect upon
modern design. These techniques freed architecture from the con-
fines of the load-bearing wall and a multitude of internal supports,
thereby allowing a freedom of internal plan and exterior design,
with an almost unlimited expanse of windows. The first steel-frame
building in Canada is believed to be the Robert Simpson Store,
erected in Toronto in 1895. In addition, an ever-expanding range of

manufactured materials challenged architects' abilities to design: decorative cast concrete, terrazzo and linoleum flooring, flexible polished metal, glass bricks, shiny black bakelite, and new plastics were among the materials now generally available.

During the early part of the century the dialogue among architects became livelier, as more publications on Canadian architecture appeared and as schools of architecture became established within the university system. The move away from architectural education based on the apprenticeship tradition, to training within a set curriculum at the university level, marked the evolution of the profession. No longer rooted in traditional artistic skills handed down from one generation to the next, architecture came to reflect a highly technical and business-oriented society. These changes helped to create a professionalism among architects that equipped them to compete with the best, world-wide.

But these advances did not on their own bring about a change of style. While architecture elsewhere in the Western world underwent its most significant upheavals in centuries, much of Canadian architecture remained wedded to tradition. One is struck by the survival of historically based architectural styles right into the middle of the century. We will see the persistence of historicism in the Beaux-Arts, Edwardian Classicism, Modern Classicism, Art Deco, Modern Gothic, and the various revival styles, some of which are popular today.

This persistence is explained by the dominance of two influences — the Arts and Crafts tradition of England and the École des Beaux-Arts of France. The former had evolved from the ideas of nineteenth-century writers and designers such as John Ruskin (1819–1900) and William Morris (1834–1896), who placed great value upon national vernacular forms. This led, in Canada as elsewhere, to the reinterpretation of older house forms (see *Revival Styles*) and to a search for ways to express Canadian nationalism in architecture. The two streams of thought were not mutually exclusive, however; one of the greatest Canadian proponents of a national style was John Lyle (1872–1945), a product of the other important tradition, the Beaux-Arts. This latter was an approach to design that stressed more rigidly systematized planning and a use of classical motifs. Both approaches made their contribution to university training in Canada, and they remained the predominant educational influences until European architects introduced the International style to North American students just before the Second World War. From that time on, nationalist aspirations were subsumed by the Internationalists' claims of universality.

Critical to the dramatic move away from historically derived styles to what we now think of as "modern" architecture, was an intellectual approach that had its roots in the nineteenth century. In Europe, certain pioneering architects had attempted a radical break with the past. While the avant-garde argued the irrelevance of historicism, other architects fought a rearguard action to reaffirm the architectural styles that had infused Western culture for two thousand years. In the end, however, abstractionism won the day. After the Second World War, the modern styles — Internationalism, Expressionism, Brutalism and later Post-Modernism — were eventually all fully accepted as the norm.

What was meant by "modern" architecture? Initially, the term implied strictly functional planning, the so-called honest expression of materials and the end of ornament. Practically, this translated into soaring, steel-and-glass towers and sleek, open-plan houses. Ideologically, this new architecture was meant to express confidence in a shining new world and an egalitarian world order. These sentiments peaked in Canada with the 1967 centennial celebrations. The site of Expo '67 in Montreal became a showcase for new architecture and a proving ground for Canada's coming-of-age. Experimental designs such as Buckminster Fuller's geodesic dome and Moshe Safdie's modular precast concrete apartment units were exciting and forward looking.

By the second half of the century, the effects of corporate finance were generally felt in the construction industry, which encouraged increasingly massive commercial developments. These were often at odds with the older, smaller-scale neighbourhoods in which they stood. In the late 1960s and the 1970s, the proliferation of tall steel-and-glass towers of predictably cubic proportions and smooth finishes evoked a reaction. There had been a noticeable decline in the quality of the urban environment and issues such as the preservation of historic architecture, energy conservation, and planning for livable urban communities became public concerns. Architects rejected the impersonalized machine aesthetic and responded to the need for a sense of privacy, individuality, and human scale by designing buildings that used more varied massing and highly textured materials. Learning from new approaches in Europe — namely the English Brutalist movement and the Dutch Structuralist movement — Canadian architects produced a variety of structures that reflected a return to a more organic approach to design and an architecture that attempted to be more sensitive to community values. These buildings, with their blocky profiles and rough walls, were dubbed Brutalist. Freed from the rigidity of the Internationalist style, other architects exploited new structural possibilities to produce buildings with highly dramatic spaces and sculptural shapes; and these buildings are sometimes called Expressionist.

During the 1980s and 1990s, concerns for the environment and the economy grew while the dream of a utopian future dimmed. Canada, along with most of the developed world, now finds itself in the process of re-examining traditional values not just for architecture, but for society in general. The Post-Modern trend in architecture reflects the attempt to use older, humanistic ideas in new ways.

In examining twentieth-century architecture, we must acknowledge that we are as yet too close to our subject to clearly distinguish the forest from the trees. With the benefit of hindsight, future critics and historians may challenge our analysis of this period. Meanwhile, the selection we have made of buildings and styles is one possible perspective on our time. The century has brought us full circle, back to the roots of much of Western architecture, to an appreciation of those values inherent in classical design and to a re-evaluation of vernacular forms. How these trends will be integrated with the lessons of the twentieth century is the challenge for the twenty-first.

The Beaux-Arts Style

Grand and theatrical, monumental and self-confident, the Beaux-Arts style dominated public and commercial architecture in the first two decades of the twentieth century. It was a classical style and so we find the full vocabulary of classical forms, such as columns, pilasters, pediments, and entablatures. But these buildings are executed on a vast scale, with monumental porticoes, intimidatingly long flights of stairs, and blindingly white stone surfaces. Usually sited at the intersections of principal streets or at the end of great vistas, they were meant to give drama to the urban scene. The sense of theatre continued inside with vast, axially planned interiors, laid out in an unfolding progression of spaces with coffered or domed ceilings and classical decoration executed in marble, coloured stones, bronze, gilding, and painting. More modest structures in the Beaux-Arts style, such as banks, commercial premises, and smaller public buildings, retain the oversized, almost bloated architectural details characteristic of the style. These smaller buildings are sometimes in brick or even wood.

The style was named for the École des Beaux-Arts in Paris from whence it came. The École reached its zenith of popularity and influence in the late nineteenth century when architects from all over Europe, Canada, and the United States came to study there. The school trained its pupils in an eclectic vocabulary of classical forms taken from antique Greece and Rome, Renaissance Italy, and eighteenth-century Neoclassical Europe. Several American faculties of architecture modelled their curricula closely upon the Parisian. Influential in the spread of the style in North America was the Universal Exposition of 1893, held in Chicago, Illinois. Built by the leading architectural firms of the day, the exposition site was a *tour-de-force* of Beaux-Arts design. Almost every structure was in the same white, theatrical style, and all the buildings were arranged harmoniously along broad avenues, complete with lakes, fountains, and sculptures. Architects and patrons alike came away from the exposition convinced that the new classicism was the style of the future.

A number of Canadian architects studied at the École des Beaux-Arts and worked in the offices of the great Beaux-Arts architects of the day. Some of the finest Beaux-Arts monuments were close at hand to study, such as the New York Public Library (1897–1911) and Grand Central Station (1907–13), and most significant architectural competitions of the day were discussed and illustrated in the great number of architectural journals available at the time, such as *American Architect and Building News*, *Canadian Architect and Builder*, and others.

71. Union Station (1919–27), 65–75 Front Street West, Toronto, Ontario (Ross and Macdonald, H.G. Jones, and John M. Lyle, architects)   Among the finest buildings in Canada in the Beaux-Arts style are the railway stations, and the most magnificent of these is Toronto Union Station. Over 750 feet long (and virtually impossible to photograph), this building exemplifies what Beaux-Arts railway

stations were meant to say: You have arrived in a great city. The axial planning of the style, with principal paths of movement clearly laid out and secondary paths leading off from them, was ideal for buildings handling large numbers of people. The exterior styling is monumental and bold and relatively severe. Inside, there is a beautifully coffered ceiling, sculptures, and rich finishing materials.

72. Château Dufresne (1916–18), 4040 Sherbrooke Street East, Montreal, Quebec (Dufresne and Renard, architects) (facing page)   The Beaux-Arts, though it was popular in other countries as a domestic style for the urban elite, never caught on in Canada. Examples like this handsome double are rare indeed. The architects have used projecting ends to frame the centre section of paired, giant columns. The landscaping, especially the arrangement of the terraces and stairs, is used to heighten the sense of monumentality.

73. Canadian Imperial Bank of Commerce (1901), corner of Front and Queen Streets, Dawson, Yukon (above) While the Beaux-Arts style was originally intended for large buildings, it worked well for smaller public and commercial buildings also, as many small-town banks and libraries attest. The features of the large buildings were simply scaled down and applied, with the same sense of gigantism of the larger buildings. Again the interiors are well finished.

74. Canadian Imperial Bank of Commerce (1906), Watson, Saskatchewan (Darling and Pearson, architects) (above) Often, prefabricated Beaux-Arts bank buildings were among the earliest structures to appear in some western Canadian communities. These buildings gave a certain dignity to the instant cities and towns of the great plains, and suggested something of their ambitions for the future. The handling of architectural details on these small, wooden buildings is the same as on the larger, brick and stone structures: giant columns, freestanding or attached, and a large-scale entablature.

75. Théâtre Montcalm (1903), Place d'Youville, Quebec City, Quebec (W.S. Painter, F.X. Berlinguet, and R.P. Lemay, architects) (facing page) As the centrepiece in an urban square, this building is as theatrical as the productions it staged. Other Beaux-Arts buildings on corner lots often used a dome as a device for accentuating the site. Here the curved mansard roof *à la parisienne* declares the very Frenchness of this design.

76. Child's Building (1909), 207–11 Portage Avenue, Winnipeg, Manitoba (demolished) (J.H.G. Russell, architect) (above) The Beaux-Arts style offered a workable solution to the problems of designing highrises. In classical design, buildings are often subdivided vertically into three zones: a short base storey that serves as a visual foundation to the design; a longer centre zone where the principal storey or storeys are located; and a shorter attic storey. This formula was used to give visual sense to the early highrises, the difference being that several storeys are included within each of the three zones. Unfortunately, this approach to design banished much of the decorative detail to the roofline, where passersby could hardly appreciate it.

The Edwardian Classical Style

Edwardian Classicism appeared in the earliest years of the twentieth century and flourished until the First World War, a period that roughly corresponds to the reign of Britain's King Edward VII. Edwardian Classical public buildings are grandiose and robustly modelled and have rich surface decoration. Favourite motifs are the "giant" orders, exuberant and asymmetrically placed cupolas or towers, imposing domes whose supports may be decorated with oversized consoles, open balustrades, and round-headed and broken pediments. Doors and windows are often framed by block or Gibbs surrounds. As the period worn on, a reaction to the extremely rich elements of the style resulted in a taste for "stripped" classicism (see *Modern Classicism*). The style was used almost exclusively for public and commercial buildings.

Like the Beaux-Arts style, the Edwardian Classical style calls for interior decoration, featuring coloured stones, gilding, plasterwork, and woodwork, all on a classical theme. The style exhibits many affinities with the monumental French Beaux-Arts style, and indeed, as the buildings themselves clearly indicate, the style was strongly influenced by the teaching and tastes of the École. The immediate source of inspiration, however, was contemporary Britain, where the architectural currents and cross-currents ranged from a revival of the grandiloquent English baroque featured in large public buildings, to the free and selective use of classical forms found in smaller structures. Edwardian Classicism diverged from the Beaux-Arts in two fundamental ways: it possessed a lingering sense of the picturesque and it deliberately avoided strict adherence to the classical rules espoused by the more formal Beaux-Arts.

In Britain, Edwardian Classicism was a response to the country's need for a national style, and for a reflection of its imperial might. Similar nationalistic sentiments induced some British-trained architects to introduce the style to Canada. In the eyes of certain Canadian architects, the Beaux-Arts had become an American style, and they hoped to counter America's spreading influence by reaffirming Canada's British affiliations. Many of these architects had been trained in the Arts and Crafts Movement, which sought to fuse arts and crafts ideals with those of revived classicism.

77. Birkbeck Building (1908-10), 8-10 Adelaide Street East, Toronto, Ontario (George W. Gouin-lock, architect) (facing page) The Birkbeck is typical of buildings erected by small financial institutions in Canada's principal cities in the early years of the twentieth century. Constructed with a steel frame and a concrete façade of grand design and eclectic sculptural decoration, it combines classical motifs with advanced modern technology.

78. The Saskatchewan Legislative Building (1907), Regina, Saskatchewan (E and W.S. Maxwell, archi-ects) (above) When it was constructed, the Legislative Building was praised for its English style, which, according to one critic, was historically more suited to Canada than the Beaux-Arts style adopted for many American state buildings. Although the details are English baroque, most notably he dome with its square drum and mannerist detailing, the building owes a great deal to Beaux-Arts design and planning. The Maxwells, who hailed from Montreal, were typical of a number of Canadian architects who tempered the English baroque with the discipline of the Beaux-Arts.

79. Post Office (1911), Moose Jaw, Saskatchewan (Department of Public Works) (facing page)
The federal government adopted a restrained version of Edwardian Classicism for its smaller public buildings and post offices. A jaunty corner cupola, well delineated cornice, strong corner quoining, pronounced keystones and voussoirs, all part of the classical vocabulary, are used freely to animate an otherwise functional building.

80. Macdonald Engineering Building (1908), McGill University, Montreal, Quebec (P.E. Nobbs, architect) (above) Percy Erskine Nobbs, an influential professor of architecture at McGill University, encouraged the adoption of contemporary British styles, modified to suit local climatic conditions. The Macdonald Engineering Building is an example of such adaptations. Its free use of abstracted architectural motifs and sheathing of grey Montreal limestone illustrate the creativity and adaptability of Edwardian Classicism.

The Chicago Style

"Chicago style" is a name that applies to certain commercial buildings of the 1890s to the 1930s. It derives from new techniques in commercial construction as this was developed in large urban centres such as Chicago at the end of the nineteenth century. The most striking visual characteristic of these multi-storey buildings is the grid-like organization of window and wall surfaces. The elevations are usually divided into three distinct zones, with a base devoted to large glass display windows, an intermediate section consisting of the bulk of the floors, and an attic storey that is often capped by a bold cornice. Decoration, usually sculpted stone or terracotta, is often concentrated at the ground on the base storey, and on the attic storey. These buildings are often clad in stone and brick, with some use of cast, artificial stone. Many large commercial buildings, like the Robert Simpson Store in Toronto (1895) or the Daly Building in Ottawa (1905), were built on this model. Winnipeg's warehouse district is a good example of how this commercial style could set the tone for an entire area of a city.

By the late nineteenth century, new building materials and new building types appeared. Significant among the new materials were steel and reinforced concrete. Although cast and wrought iron had been in use for some time, it was the development and commercial availability of the stronger and more fire-resistant steel and concrete that ultimately changed both the way buildings were constructed and the way they looked. Their effect was first seen, in a consistent way, in Chicago. A devastating fire in 1871 had almost levelled the young city. Faced with the need for fast, massive rebuilding in the urban core, and rising real estate values, architects designed increasingly tall buildings that provided the maximum possible rentable space on a site. Architects like Louis Sullivan (1856–1924) designed buildings whose exterior walls acted more like protective skins stretched over an internal skeleton. Since these exterior walls were no longer load-bearing, window areas could be expanded to provide improved interior ventilation and illumination. The divisions between the windows lost much of their three-dimensional mass, while the glazed areas gained in size and prominence. These were often arranged as extending bays or as large sheets of plate glass flanked by narrower, movable side-lights, which design became known as Chicago windows.

Improved structural steel framing along with the perfection of the electric elevator allowed the construction of increasingly tall buildings, which became especially popular in urban cores where high densities brought correspondingly high real estate costs. The skyscraper derives from these early Chicago-style buildings; it has, however, survived through many stylistic changes to become the norm for commercial urban structures in the twentieth century.

81. The Trapp Building (1912–13), 668 Columbia Street, New Westminster, British Columbia (Gardiner, Mercer and Gardiner, architects) (page 126, following)
The large area of glass on the façade of this commercial building is typical of Chicago style design. It allowed the maximum amount of daylight into the work area at a time when efficient electrical lighting was not always available. The building's solid, blank side walls presumed the construction of similarly scaled neighbours that would screen them from view. The façade is ornamented with terracotta tile in a classical revival motif typical of the treatment of many large office buildings of this era.

82. The Union Bank Building (1903-04), 504 Main Street, Winnipeg, Manitoba (Darling and Pearson, architects) (page 127, following)
This steel-frame building was faced with brick and terracotta. It exhibits the typical division of the façade into three zones, with a double-storey base, tiers of intermediary storeys, and a heavily embellished attic storey. The relatively large amount of wall surface in proportion to the window area is, however, a conservative treatment.

83. The Daly Building (1905), Rideau Street, Ottawa, Ontario (Moses C. Edey, architect) (above)
Demolished by the National Capital Commission in 1992, this building reflects the fate of many fine
early Chicago-style buildings whose business-like severity the public have found difficult to love. This
photograph, taken during demolition, clearly shows the grid-like framework of steel and concrete
that carried the weight of the building and allowed for large areas of glass to hang between the supporting elements.

**84. The Confederation Building (1912), 457 Main Street, Winnipeg, Manitoba (J. Wilson Gray, archi-
tect) (facing page)**   This steel-frame structure rises ten storeys on a reinforced concrete foundation.
It was constructed to provide offices for the Confederation Life Insurance Company as well as for
various professional tenants. As a prestige property, it was elaborately finished with marble, copper,
and oak on the interior public spaces, and with terracotta and polished granite on the exterior. The
division of its façade into three distinct zones and its large tripartite windows are typical features of
the Chicago style, while the curved façade is an idiosyncratic response to its awkward site.

85. The Canada Building (1912–13), 105 21st Street East, Saskatoon, Saskatchewan (James Chisholm and Sons, architects) (above)   Prominently sited on a downtown corner lot, this was a prestigious building in its day. Its ground-floor display windows have been altered, but the building retains much of its fine terracotta detailing, including two large buffalo heads just over the main entry.

86. McCallum-Hill Building (1912), 1876 Scarth Street, Regina, Saskatchewan (Edgar Storey and William Van Egmond, architects) (facing page)   This is a classic example of the Chicago style in Canada. Its tripartite exterior organization, the overhanging cornice, the Chicago windows, and the application of conservative decorative elements are typical of the cautious interpretation of the style in small-to-medium sized cities. Note the survival of the old fire escape.

The Modern Classical Style

Many features of Modern Classicism, a style popular in the 1920s and 1930s, strike us as similar to the Beaux-Arts. Here again are large public buildings following the classical theme. They have symmetrical main façades, flat or nearly flat roofs, a monumental order of pilasters (but no columns) across the front, and prominent plinths and entablatures, all executed in white stone or artifical cast stone. Sometimes the classical motifs of pilasters and entablatures are extremely simplified, so that the surface of the building is a grid of horizontal and vertical lines. Smaller public buildings are often faced with brick, with contrasting stone trim. The execution is quite different in that the classical features have been flattened and linearized, as though the building's façade were reduced to a line drawing, rather than being something three dimensional. Where the Beaux-Arts is theatrical and sumptuous, modern classicism is dignified and restrained. It was a serviceable style for public buildings of all kinds.

Inside, the floor plans are usually symmetrical, arranged along a central axis. The finishing details are less rich than those we would find in a Beaux-Arts interior. The floors are wood, tile, linoleum, or terrazzo, with marble reserved for entrance lobbies. Walls and ceilings are plainly painted or tiled. The emphasis inside is on economy, efficiency, and sanitary convenience.

Modern Classicism was a child of its time as much as it was the progeny of the Beaux-Arts. The flamboyance and ostentation of the early twentieth century were replaced by post–First World War sobriety. Architects trained in the Beaux-Arts style of the pre-war years found that they and their clients wanted something more restrained, and in the 1920s this abbreviated classicism is what they constructed. Then in 1929 the stock market crash halted construction almost entirely. When federal, provincial, and municipal governments started makework projects in the 1930s as a stimulus to the economy, the buildings that they commissioned were purposely frugal in character: handsome, conservatively classical designs, with no waste of the taxpayer's money. The largest patron of architecture in the 1920s and 1930s was the federal government, particularly after the passing of the Public Works Construction Act of 1934. The federal Department of Public Works built a number of sizeable, multipurpose federal buildings in larger cities, as well as smaller post offices, customs and excise offices, and various other buildings in towns and villages. Governments at the provincial and municipal levels erected office buildings and city halls in the Modern Classical style. While Modernism had truly begun in Europe (see *International Style*), Canadian architects and their clients were unable or unwilling as yet to abandon the historical revival styles that had served them so well.

87. City Hall (1935–36), 453 West 12th Avenue, Vancouver, British Columbia (Townley and Matheson, architects) (above) Modern Classical public buildings were similar in design, whatever their specific purpose and wherever they were erected. The exteriors were either white or a neutral, buff-coloured stone. One finds occasionally elements in artificial stone, particularly cast decorative pieces. The façades have the vocabulary of classical features, such as the orders and classical mouldings, but these features are highly stylized, flattened, and abbreviated. Occasionally there is some decorative sculpture, such as a coat of arms, over the entrance or in the centre of the entablature.

88. Federal Building (1935–37), 1975 Scarth Street, Regina, Saskatchewan (Reilly and Portnall, architects) (facing page, top) Though modern classicism was a style of restraint, it could also be a style of imaginative design. Here the architect of a medium-sized public building has inverted some of the rules of classical design: note the rounded corners on the ground floor and the cutaway upper corners of the building. Where the entranceway of most classical buildings projects, this one recedes. The pale brick works well in combination with the stone. While the classicism of this design still predominates, one can see certain affinities with the Moderne style.

89. Federal Building (1934–36), 98 Victoria Street, Amherst, Nova Scotia (Leslie R. Fairn, architect) (facing page, bottom)   Bold and simple, the order of giant columns supporting a wide, plain entablature was an excellent solution for public buildings, large and small. This is a fairly late date for such a pure, Beaux-Arts building, signalling the preference for conservative design in public-sector commissions.

90. Bank of Montreal (1930–34), 144 Wellington Street, Ottawa, Ontario (Ernest I. Barott, architect) (above) Modern classicism could give small buildings a tremendous sense of monumentality by relatively simple means. The architect uses giant pilasters several storeys high, leading up to a mammoth entablature. The surfaces are smooth and serve as a blank foil for the sculptural panels. These panels are worth close examination, for they are nationalistic and didactic in their themes.

91. Town Hall (1912–13), 430 Main Street, Melville, Saskatchewan (Storey and Van Egmond, architects) (above) Modern classicism in its most reduced and economical form still provided dignity to modest structures. Note how the brick pilasters are reduced to mere panels, leading up to a simple entablature. The classical forms are so simplified that it is a moot point whether the stylistic influence is Modern Classicism or the Georgian Revival style.

The Art Deco Style

The Art Deco style of the late 1920s and the 1930s was the last of the great decorative styles. The decorative motifs chosen were from many cultures and many historical periods. Readily recognizable are the pilasters and entablatures of classical architecture. Less obvious are the motifs from ancient Egyptian and pre-Columbian cultures, such as pyramids and ziggurats. There are naturalistic themes: animals, flowers, rainbows, fountains, and waves. Additionally there are references to the glories of the machine age in portrayals of bridges, gushing oil wells, steamships, and airplanes. Many motifs are simply geometrical, including zigzags, chevrons, stripes, and spirals. The true spirit of Art Deco, though, lay in its stylized treatment of these decorative devices. Everything is flattened and streamlined and has an air of stylishness and breathless speed that makes this architecture seem the very embodiment of the Jazz Age.

We find a variety of buildings in the Art Deco style, but especially noteworthy are the new highrises that were then beginning to punctuate the skylines of Canadian cities. Art Deco was stylishly popular for commercial properties, especially big department stores. A few banks and government buildings of the time were also built in the Art Deco style. Overall, their designs are classical in their symmetry, use of motifs, mouldings, and proportions, but such buildings sometimes had specifically Canadian themes, such as buffalo heads, Indians, Mounties, beavers, trains, and scenes from Canadian history. These motifs were executed in stone, cast stone, bronze, and steel. Interior materials include marbles, black glass, terrazzo, fine wood, and more bronze and steel. Murals and historical paintings were often included in the designs.

Art Deco was named for the *Exposition universale des arts décoratifs et industriels modernes* held in Paris in 1925. This was the event that brought the style — intended as much for furnishings and *objets d'arts* as for architecture — into public view. Art Deco quickly became popular in North America. We find many Art Deco motifs employed on Frank Lloyd Wright's structures, particularly his rambling, asymmetrical prairie houses (see the *Prairie Style*). Other architects appended Art Deco motifs to the skyscrapers that were just then being built in large numbers in American cities. The shape of skyscraper design was set in New York City, where a city bylaw required tall buildings to be stepped back on their upper storeys to allow air and light to penetrate to street level. The resulting ziggurat-like quality of these structures seemed tailor-made for the Art Deco style, although often the best decoration was applied to the topmost storeys, where it could not possibly be seen from the street. Canadian architects had ample opportunity to study examples of Art Deco design. They saw these buildings on their travels, and also saw them widely published both in architectural journals and in the popular press. As well, Art Deco design provided a fashionable backdrop for many Hollywood films.

92. Marine Building (1929–30), 355 Burrard Street, Vancouver, British Columbia (McCarter and Nairne, architects) (facing page) One of the most delightful Art Deco buildings in the country is the Marine Building. It typifies the application of decorative detail to the skyscraper type. Notice the beauty and intricacy of the sculpted details around the main door. This building is definitely worth a visit since the interior is a rich display of the Art Deco style.

93. City Delivery Building (1939–40), 16 Bay Street, Toronto, Ontario (Charles B. Dolphin, architect) Startlingly avant-garde for the usually stodgy Department of Public Works, the City Delivery Building exemplifies what modernity and simplicity could achieve together. Here there is a classical

theme in the flattened pilasters that separate the vertical banks of windows. Yet to either side are bands of windows that wrap around the corners of the building, in defiance of all of the classical rules of design. This building has some wonderful Art Deco sculpture, including reliefs of airplanes and ships.

94. Bessborough Armoury (1932–33), 2025 West 11th Avenue, Vancouver, British Columbia (R.T. Perry, architect) (facing page) Most armouries built by the Department of National Defence were designed in one of the medieval styles — Romanesque Revival or Tudor Revival — reminiscent of the fortresses and castles of medieval Europe. But here we have an unusual example of the Art Deco. The architect has employed the flat, vertical lines of Art Deco to suggest something of the verticality of medieval design, such as we have seen already in the Gothic Revival styles.

95. Cormier House (1930), 1418 Avenue des Pins West, Montreal, Quebec (E. Cormier, architect) (above) The few private houses designed in the Art Deco style were built for the urban avant-garde. Architect Cormier's house for himself is beautiful, albeit lacking in the cozy charm that Canadians seem to prefer in their dwellings. Note the vertical linearism and the flat, blank spaces that serve as a foil for the focus of interest around the door and around the long window at one side.

96. Bank of Nova Scotia (1929–30), Prince and Hollis Streets, Halifax, Nova Scotia (John M. Lyle, architect) (above) As Art Deco buildings go, this is an extremely conservative example; the Art Deco styling can be seen in the sculptural details around the openings and inside. The conservatism of the design — the classical symmetry, division of storeys, pilasters and entablature — were chosen by the architect so that the building would be sympathetic to Province House, a Palladian Style building dating from 1811–18, across the street. This kind of sensitivity to setting was not all that common in the early twentieth century, and was one of the aspects of Lyle's work that signalled its superiority. Like many commercial buildings of the time, this one has a steel frame.

97. Balfour Building (1930), 119–21 Spadina Avenue, Toronto, Ontario (Benjamin Brown, architect) (facing page) More run-of-the-mill buildings such as smaller office buildings, warehouses, or apartment buildings could use Art Deco styling successfully, although the details were reserved for the areas around the doors and along rooflines. Some of the great, unsung examples of the style are to be found in the warehouse districts of our cities, or well up above eye level in commercial areas. Look up!

The Moderne Style

Flat roofs, clean white surfaces, aerodynamic shapes, windows flush to the wall and sometimes wrapping around corners, chrome tubing, and sleek, horizontal stripes of applied metal mark the Moderne as a style that celebrates the aesthetics of the machine age. Popular from the 1920s until about 1945, this eclectic style borrows its taste for simplicity, smooth surfaces, and asymmetrical balance from the nascent modernism of European avant-garde architects, but without completely shunning ornament. Moderne architecture shares with its sibling, the Art Deco style, a preference for reflective materials, particularly on interior public spaces, so that highly polished wood veneers and new, manufactured materials such as polished metal, frosted glass, glossy black bakelite, glass blocks, and tube neon lighting provide an exciting luminescence.

The popularity of mass-produced materials reflected a convergence of architecture and industrial design. The celebration of bare, unadorned surfaces, whose attraction lay in the simple beauty of frankly expressed materials and simplicity of form, set Moderne architecture apart from the highly decorative Art Deco Style. In Canada, the aerodynamic forms with rounded corners and horizontal massing accentuated by applied "speed-stripe" markings and the flat roof were especially popular for commercial buildings such as shops, restaurants, gas stations, and bus depots, as well as for industrial developments. A few daring house owners also enjoyed the sleek modern shapes and sunny interiors of this style, also sometimes known as "depression modern," "horizontal deco," or "streamlined moderne."

98. The former Toronto, Hamilton and Buffalo Railway Station (1931–33), Hamilton, Ontario (Fell-heimer and Wagner, architects) (above) This railway station is a radical departure from the classically inspired norm for most large Canadian stations, a change of style probably due to the American architects who designed it. Instead of a rather dated classicism, there are strip windows, rounded corners, and a decorative use of slick, polished metal expressing the contemporary fascination with industrial design.

99. The Thomson Building (1939), Timmins, Ontario (H. Sheppard and G. Masson, architects) (above) This combined newspaper office and broadcasting station was erected for future communications magnate Roy Thomson. The use of stucco and glass bricks, the minimal ornamentation, the sleek, curving surfaces, the banded windows, and the flat roof are all hallmarks of the Moderne — a style particularly suited to this monument to technology.

100. Alexandra Bar (1940), Drumheller, Alberta (B. Holoston and Jim Parsons, builders) (facing page, top)   This relatively small building is a late but classic example of the streamlined shapes favoured in the Moderne style. The sleek, horizontal profile and curved surfaces impart an air of smart sophistication to the business. The building was restored and renovated under the Drumheller Main Street Project in 1987–89.

101. The Garage Roadhouse, Wolfville, Nova Scotia (facing page, bottom)
This former gas station has been renovated to serve as a restaurant. Above the new canopy one can still distinguish the "speed-stripe" that accentuates the sweep of the rounded corner and the flat roof.

The Twentieth Century Revival Styles

Buildings traditionally have been divided into two kinds — the architect designed, and the self-built or vernacular. By the twentieth century, however, many societies, including Canada, had become extensively industrialized and, with the move to more mechanized and capitalized economies, few people continued to build for their own use along established, traditional lines. Nevertheless, the desire for tradition is a resilient sentiment. Many people prefer to live and work in buildings that provide some sense of continuity with familiar and comfortable beliefs and forms, whatever avant-garde designers may say. Consequently, we have alongside the "modern" movement in twentieth-century architecture a sturdy and enduring line of historically based styles, known as the revival styles. These forms provide contemporary buildings with a traditional clothing, and they have become the twentieth-century equivalent of vernacular architecture, even though they may be designed by professional architects or contractors. We find many houses in these styles in suburbs of the 1990s.

In Canada, there are several revival styles, all deriving from architecture of one past age or another, either European or North American. Thus, we have period revivals of the Tudor era, as well as colonial-era revivals that include the architecture of the European colonizers — in particular, that of the English, the French, and the Spanish. Sometimes, elements from these different traditions are mixed in one building. Revival style buildings can be distinguished from their architectural ancestors by their tendency to eclecticism, together with the use of contemporary building materials and subtle differences in scale and proportion.

The Georgian Revival Style

The Georgian Revival Style is by far the most popular of the twentieth-century revival styles. It appeared in the 1910s and is still going strong today. Most commonly used in domestic design, it is a classical style distinguished by a symmetrical façade with a decorative focus on a central doorway. This entrance is often flanked by sidelights and topped by a fanlight, or a curved or broken pediment. Sometimes the main entry is sheltered by a columned porch. Other typical motifs include multi-pane sash windows, a front-sloping pitched or gambrel roof, and eaves ornamented with dentils. Walls may be faced with wooden clapboarding, brick, stone, or even stucco.

The style imitates English and Dutch colonial architecture built during the reigns of the English Georges (eighteenth and early nineteenth centuries), especially as it appeared in the American colonies. It was first revived in the United States during the late nineteenth century, when Beaux-Arts trained architects such as McKim, Mead, and White built large mansions in this manner for wealthy clients along the eastern seaboard. During the 1920s, the style was popularized by certain historic restorations, specifically that of colonial Williamsburg. Influential also was the work of certain British architects at the beginning of the twentieth century, in particular Richard Norman Shaw's house designs, which were a form of revived, eighteenth-century classicism. In Canada, the style was initially popular in the Atlantic provinces and in Ontario, although it has since made its appearance across the country and continues to offer inspiration for much suburban development.

102. 32 Range Road (1930), Ottawa, Ontario (W.E. Noffke, architect) (above)
This house evokes the classically inspired stone homesteads erected throughout the Ottawa Valley and the Rideau Canal corridor. Its relatively plain and strictly symmetrical façade focuses on the door, which has sidelights and a toplight. There is also a bull's eye window. Note also the reduced window size on the second floor, pitch-roofed dormers, and prominent end chimneys, suggesting that the architect was thoroughly acquainted with local vernacular forms.

103. Provincial Court House (1928), 301 Prairie Street N.E., Weyburn, Saskatchewan (Maurice Sharon, architect) (above) The use of brick and white-painted wood trim imitates the Colonial Revival style restorations of colonial Williamsburg. The relieving arches around the ground-floor windows imitate American architecture of the revolutionary era, while the relatively elaborate detailing, such as the prominent keystones, the dentils under the eaves, and the tracery in the upper windows, show the influence of the more formal Beaux-Arts design on this style.

The Tudor Revival Style

The Tudor Revival style was also very popular for houses, although one also finds some small commercial structures and churches using its motifs. The style is most readily recognized by the use of mock half-timbering, that is, exposed wooden beams infilled with stucco. Other typical motifs include drip moulding, leaded glass, bay and oriel windows, twisted chimney-pots, prominent gables, steeply pitched and irregular rooflines, and a generally picturesque, asymmetrical massing.

This style draws its inspiration from the rural vernacular architecture of Tudor England. The nineteenth-century English Arts and Crafts movement had greatly admired the pre-industrial, medieval crafts, especially those used in the building trade, and devotees such as Philip Webb (1831–1915) and C.F.A. Voysey (1875–1941) based some of their domestic designs upon medieval precursors. This movement found supporters in North America, where nostalgia for the past and an admiration of things British fostered the transatlantic development of this revival. It was especially popular in certain affluent suburbs of Toronto, Vancouver, and Victoria. Its associations with domesticity have ensured its continued popularity. Where classical elements are included with the medieval, as is often found on public schools of the period, a so-called Jacobean variant results.

104. 27 Clemow Avenue (1929), Ottawa, Ontario (W.E. Noffke, architect) (facing page, top)
The use of half-timbered gables, twisted chimney-pots, leaded windows, drip moulding, and wrought ironwork lend a romantic air to this house, while its relatively small scale and horizontal massing capture the feeling of the 1920s. The picturesque qualities of this charming house are enhanced by its setting at the edge of an informally planned park.

105. Brock House (1913), Point Grey, Vancouver, British Columbia (Maclure and Fox, architects) (facing page, bottom) The steeply pitched roof, prominent chimneys, and mock half-timbering are hallmarks of the Tudor Revival style. The architectural firm of Maclure and Fox built several homes in this manner for well-to-do patrons in Vancouver and Victoria, and one will find such houses in wealthy, older suburbs across the country.

The Spanish Colonial Revival Style

Popular from the 1910s to the 1940s, this style was used for houses, small commercial buildings, and a few movie houses. It is identified by the use of smooth stucco walls, gently pitched red tile or pseudo-tile roofs, arched doorways and window openings, covered porches, and curvilinear gables. These visual characteristics recall the architecture of the Spanish colonizers of the American Southwest, and it was there, towards the end of the nineteenth century, that the style was first revived in designs for large mansions and hotels. By the 1910s, its use had spread to more modest structures across the United States and Canada.

In California, the style was appropriate to the climate and also rooted in local history. The rustic qualities of adobe and wood (despite the fact that concrete and stucco almost always substituted for adobe) also satisfied the fashion for unpretentious materials. This taste for apparent simplicity derived from the English Arts and Crafts Movement. Concrete manufacturers saw the style as an ideal vehicle for their product, and many construction magazines in the United States and Canada featured articles concerning the economic advantages of concrete construction. In practice, stucco applied over wood remained a more economical alternative in Canada.

The Spanish Revival Style has a number of siblings, including the simpler Mission (or Pueblo) style as well as the more formal Mediterranean style. Mission style buildings favour flat roofs with stepped parapets, rectangular openings, and a rough wall finish in closer imitation of handmade adobe. The Mediterranean style, on the other hand, borrows not only from Spanish architecture but also from Moorish and Italian design, and was popularized in the 1920s by its use for grand homes built as winter retreats in Florida resorts such as Palm Beach. Canadian houses in this mode tend to be two or more storys high, with sedately symmetrical façades, balustraded piazzas, balconies, and columned entries.

106. Capitol Theatre (1928), 509–517 3rd Avenue West, Prince Rupert, British Columbia (W. Dodd and Company, architects) (facing page)   The Spanish Colonial Revival style was immensely popular in the design of cinemas during the 1920s and 1930s. This building opened in 1928 as a combined vaudeville theatre and movie house, and continued to function as a cinema until 1981 when it was renovated as a mini-mall. Its air of fantasy and its associations with California were entirely suitable for a movie house. The building suggests its mediterranean connection with red tiling and stylized classical decorative motifs.

107. Former Fire Station No. 10 (1920), 260 Sunnyside Avenue, Ottawa, Ontario (Werner Ernst Noffke, architect) (above) A fantastical structure to find on a suburban Canadian street, this fire station is an evocation of the American Southwest. The red tile roof, stucco cladding, and a prominent curved gable are all motifs borrowed from the Spanish colonial era.

The Quebec Revival Style

The Quebec Revival Style, which first appeared in the 1920s and has remained popular until today, is inspired by traditional Quebec domestic architecture. It is identified by the use of multi-pane casement windows, dormer windows, stone- or stucco-faced exterior walls, and a steeply pitched front-sloping roof with bellcast eaves, which sometimes extend to create a porch across the length of the façade.

The revival of interest in Quebec vernacular architecture originated with the Faculty of Architecture of the University of McGill in Montreal during the 1920s. Encouraged by their professors, students surveyed and produced measured drawings of old Quebec houses. Spurred by a sense of nationalism and by the revival of other colonial styles, architects began to use their knowledge of indigenous vernacular types to produce modern interpretations of the *maison Québécoise*. Sometimes the Quebec elements were mixed with motifs more typical of French or English architecture to produce a "Canadian" version. Such buildings tend also to be faced with stone or sometimes with brick, but have more steeply pitched, hipped roofs without bellcast eaves, and include dormer windows that break the eave line.

108. Maison du jardinier (1922), 1240 chemin Bord-du-lac, Dorval, Quebec (Nobbs and Hyde, architects) (above)   This romantic gardener's house is part of the grounds of a large estate. The low-pitched front-sloping roof with bellcast eaves is a hallmark of the Quebec Revival style, while the decorative embellishments distinguish it from the original Quebec style, which was relatively plain.

109. Rideau Branch Public Library (1933–34), 377 Rideau Street, Ottawa, Ontario (J.P. MacLaren, architect) (above) This small public building is distinguished by a steep hipped roof and an ornate central frontispiece. These forms, as well as the building's brick facing, suggest Jacobean and Norman design and illustrate the attempt to amalgamate French and English motifs into a new "Canadian" style.

The Arts and Crafts Movement

While the Arts and Crafts Movement influenced a great deal of architecture of the period, there is one kind of house that stands out as particularly characteristic of the movement. The houses of the Arts and Crafts Movement were wonderfully informal and unpretentious, sophisticated in a very subtle way. They were low to the ground, asymmetrical, with steeply pitched roofs. Often these houses were covered with stucco; sometimes they were even built of poured concrete meant to imitate stucco. Their surfaces were plain in the extreme, ornamented only with banks of casement windows. The eaves overhang in a picturesque manner, and the roofing material is sometimes imitation thatch. Built in the 1920s and 1930s, these houses did not find widespread popularity, as did the Georgian and Tudor Revivals, but one sees them in older suburbs, especially in British Columbia.

The Arts and Crafts Movement was an approach to architectural design rather than an architectural style *per se.* The movement, spearheaded by certain English architects such as C.F.A. Voysey and Edwin Lutyens, revived the vernacular forms of English rural domestic architecture. Their designs stressed informal, functional plans, fairly spare decoration that suggested handcraftsmanship, and a harmony with the setting that recalls the Picturesque Movement of the nineteenth century. While the ideas of these architects influenced architecture generally in the early twentieth century, these houses are the most characteristic products of their school of thought.

110. Fred H. Booth House (1922), 50 Goulburn Avenue, Ottawa, Ontario (Charles J. Saxe, architect) (facing page, bottom)   A prettified, English-vernacular cottage, this house features stucco walls, soft-looking imitation-thatch roofs, and banks of casement windows typical of the Arts and Crafts Movement. The round tower, suggestive of a Château-style tower, or a dovecote or windmill, was not often found on such houses.

111. W.F. Hunting House (1912), 3689 Angus Drive, Vancouver, British Columbia (facing page top) The steeply pitched roofline of this large house creates dramatic angles, accentuated by the smooth stucco finish. The enjoyment of geometric form is further underscored by the banks of windows, prominent chimneys, and restrained decorative elements. An important aspect of these houses is the very English style garden that surrounds them.

The Modern Gothic Style

After declining in popularity at the end of the nineteenth century, the Gothic Revival received a new lease on life in the early years of the twentieth century as the appropriate style for universities, colleges, schools, and other institutions of learning. Less often it was used for apartment buildings, highrise office buildings, and commercial rows. These large and sometimes complex buildings usually followed the Beaux-Arts system of axial, ordered planning, and are noted for the clarity and precision of their overall design. In appearance they have little in common with the High Victorian Gothic buildings. Instead, the salient features of the style are long, low symmetrical masses; crenellated towers; and distinctively Gothic fenestration, which may include oriel or bay windows. The emphasis is upon a calm, disciplined monumentality. Many of these buildings are supported by a hidden steel framing system, which gives them a subtly different appearance from the older, load-bearing walls of the High Victorian Gothic. Gone also is the polychromy of nineteenth-century Gothic Revival, to be replaced by monochrome limestone or brick.

It is possible to trace Modern Gothic back to England in the 1880s, to a small group of architects who objected to the eclectic "muscularity" of High Victorian Gothic. They looked back to the Perpendicular style of the late Middle Ages for inspiration. The flexible English Perpendicular Gothic was particularly popular, partly because it could be easily abstracted and harmonized with modern building materials. By the start of the twentieth century, the style had been adopted for important university buildings in the United States, including buildings at Princeton and Yale. From there the style came to Canada in the first decade of the twentieth century. Within its chosen fields, it enjoyed widespread popularity until the 1930s.

112. Hart House, 7 Hart House Circle (1911–19), University of Toronto, Toronto, Ontario (Henry Sproatt and Ernest Rolph, architects) (above) Designed in the great tradition of England's medieval universities, Oxford and Cambridge, Hart House is a highly sophisticated, full-blown example of a Modern Gothic building. The salient features of its style are a low, horizontal line, strong massing, and muted Gothic motifs. Built around an interior quadrangle, its various facilities are clearly planned according to Beaux-Arts principles. Hart House was a gift from Vincent Massey; it is the social, cultural, and recreational centre of the university.

113. Saskatchewan Hall (1910), University of Saskatchewan, Saskatoon, Saskatchewan (Brown and Vallance, architects) (above) Saskatchewan Hall is part of a group of Modern Gothic buildings that comprises the original campus of the University of Saskatchewan. The first president and board of directors studied the design of several universities in the United States and Canada before producing the master plan. The buildings were constructed with reinforced concrete faced in a locally quarried greystone. Situated in a pleasantly landscaped setting, the campus evokes the atmosphere of a medieval university and provides the students with a quiet academic environment.

114. St. Andrew's United Church (1912), Moose Jaw, Saskatchewan (facing page)
By comparison with High Victorian Gothic churches, Modern Gothic Revival churches have simple straightforward outlines and are usually constructed in a uniform colour of stone or brick. Most churches like St. Andrew's were inspired by the English Perpendicular of the late Middle Ages. The soaring height of the tower, the emphasis on flat wall surfaces, and large windows are characteristic of the style.

115. Victoria Rifles Armoury (1934), Cathcart Street, Montreal, Quebec (Jerome Spence, architect) (above)   Since the first permanent armouries were constructed for the militia in the 1860s, Canada's volunteer soldiers have preferred armouries that evoke the appearance of a medieval fortress. The modern Gothic style of the Cathcart Armoury suits the busy central Montreal location surprisingly well. The features that distinguish it from nineteenth-century Gothic Revival prototypes are the monochromatic stone wall, the tall wide windows with slender mullions, and the almost flat Tudor arch of the doorway.

116. Centre Block, Parliament Hill (1916–27), Ottawa, Ontario (John A. Pearson, architect, J. O. Marchand, associate architect) (above) This building replaced the original Centre Block, which was severely damaged by fire in 1916. Designed in a monumental style, the clearly articulated exterior, with its grand public entrance through the Peace Tower and flanking entrances to the House of Commons and Senate lobbies, reflects a rational and well-ordered interior plan, a hallmark of many Modern Gothic buildings. The Centre Block is the heart of the Canadian government, where the debate and passage of legislation is carried out.

The Prairie Style

The Prairie style of the 1910s, 1920s and 1930s refers to buildings that have low, horizontal proportions; flat or gently pitched roofs extending beyond the walls in deep, projecting eaves; and rectangular windows whose glazing bars form angular, geometric patterns. The flowing, informal floor plans of Prairie Style houses often include porches and terraces that extend into surrounding gardens. Plain materials like stucco and brick are preferred for exterior walls, with strips of natural wood, and occasionally stained glass inserted in windows as restrained decorative elements.

The style's horizontal emphasis reflects its origins in the flat plains of the American Midwest for which it was named. An essentially North American development, Prairie style buildings exhibit an abstract cubic massing that parallels contemporary European developments in modern architecture, while its emphasis on natural materials recalls the English Arts and Crafts Movement. The Prairie style rejects the use of historically derived ornament, expressing instead a Japanese-inspired taste for simple, clean lines, natural materials, and a close relationship to the landscape. Since the American architect Frank Lloyd Wright (1869–1959) was the style's main progenitor, buildings of this type are sometimes also called "Wrightian."

Prairie style architecture spread to Canada through the publication of house plans in magazines such as *House Beautiful*, and through the work of Canadian architects such as Francis C. Sullivan (1882–1929). Sullivan worked for a time for Wright before returning home to practise in the Ottawa area. The Canadian version of the style resulted in somewhat smaller, more compact buildings with a closer balance between verticals and horizontals. Sullivan's houses do exhibit, however, flat wall planes, simple wood detailing, overhanging eaves, and an almost complete lack of historicizing ornament. Many other Canadian architects and builders were also influenced by the style. The increasingly popular bungalow, with its deep eaves, smooth stucco or brick walls, and ground-hugging characteristics, shows its debt to the Prairie Style.

117. 166 Huron Street (1915), Ottawa, Ontario (Francis Sullivan, architect) (above)
Designed by an admirer and former associate of Frank Lloyd Wright, this building makes use of clear, geometric shapes both in its massing and in its decorative details. These qualities, in combination with the broad, sheltering eaves, reveal Sullivan's debt to the Prairie Style. The compact plan is typical of the Canadian version of the style.

118. Natatorium (1932), Moose Jaw, Saskatchewan (H. Hargreaves and N.L. Thompson, architects) (above) The spreading, rectanglar massing and low-pitched, overhanging roof of this public building show the influence of the Prairie style, while combining other stylistic motifs such as mock Tudor half-timbering and a prominent central doorway elaborated with the stylized devices typical of Art Deco design.

119. Horticulture Building (1914), Lansdowne Park, Ottawa, Ontario (Francis Sullivan, architect) (above) Designed as a horticultural display space on the grounds of the Central Canada Exhibition, this building shows the influence of Frank Lloyd Wright's early work in the juxtaposition of cleanly defined cubic masses and in the use of a flat roof with cantilevered eaves. The geometric placement of the windows and the restrained treatment of the decorative brickwork are typical of the disciplined and unified approach in Prairie-style design.

120. Caserne No. 1 (1914), 4300 rue Notre Dame est, Montreal, Quebec (Marius Defresne, architect) (above) This combined firehall and police station shows the hallmarks of the Prairie style in its strong horizontals and geometric massing. It is possible that a former student of Frank Lloyd Wright working for Dufresne was influential in introducing "Wrightian" design motifs to Montreal in this building.

121. Church of Jesus Christ of the Latter Day Saints (1913–23), Cardston, Alberta (H. Pope and H. Burton, architects) (above)   This highly original building suggests something of the Central American temples of the Mayan peoples that Wright often used for his decorative motifs. Characteristic of the style are the tall, vertical slit windows set between projecting piers, the chevron motifs, and the grid pattern of the window mullions. This building shows the close relationship between the Prairie style and Art Deco.

The International Style

The International style, popular in Canada from the 1940s to the present, is most easily recognized by its use of a module, usually a square or a rectangle, that forms the basis of a building's design. Hard, angular edges, severely plain surfaces, and large expanses of glass express a structural system based on a skeleton of steel or reinforced concrete. At its best, it is a style of subtlety, relying for its beauty upon harmonious proportions and beautifully finished materials; at its worst it is tiresomely repetitive and cheap looking. This was the style being used almost exclusively by the commercial sector in the second half of the twentieth century. It was less often used in domestic design, but where it is found, the framing system may be a traditional wood one. However, the flat roof, cube-like or rectangular massing, large, horizontally arranged windows, and lack of applied decoration maintain the severe functional qualities of the style.

This style, originally known simply as "modern," was popularized "International" by Henry-Russell Hitchcock and Philip Johnson through their catalogue for an exhibition of new work by contemporary architects at the Museum of Modern Art in New York in 1932 entitled "The International Style: Architecture Since 1922." Centres of modern design, most notably the Bauhaus in Germany, sought a new way of building that was independent of historical styles and reflective of the steel and reinforced concrete construction methods. New structural systems, they argued, demanded a new aesthetic. These systems allowed supports to be widely spaced and distributed throughout a structure, so that the exterior walls no longer bore the load of the building. They became "curtains" that could, if desired, be constructed almost entirely of glass. When leaders of this movement, such as Walter Gropius (1883–1969) and Mies Van der Rohe (1886–1969), fled Nazi Germany in the 1930s they brought the style to Britain and to North America.

Although there were examples of International style buildings erected in Canada as early as the 1930s, it was not until after the Second World War that the style took firm hold here. The ahistorical nature of Internationalism and its implied faith in a new egalitarian world order suited postwar optimism. The prosperity of the 1950s and 1960s led to a building boom that transformed Canadian cities, giving them many large commercial complexes in the style. Certain architect-designed homes also reflected the reductionism of the International style, in their openly expressed grid-like framing, unadorned curtain walls, and open, flexible interior plans. Variations on the rectangular grid included the use of other pure geometric forms such as the circle and the parabola.

122. The Mechanical Engineering Building (1948), University of Toronto, Toronto, Ontario (All-ward and Gouinlock, architects) (above) This early example of the International style in Canada uses the severe planar surface, cubic massing, and strip windows set flush to the wall surface, which are all hallmarks of the early International style.

123. Via Rail Station (1966), 200 Tremblay Road, Ottawa, Ontario (J.B. Parkin and Associates, architects) (above and facing page)   A later version of the International style, this building uses exposed steel trusswork and a frank expression of supporting elements combined in an elegant minimalist *tour de force*. The refined design of these supporting pillars have become part of the decorative program in this structure. The sweeping curves of the staircase leading from the grand hall to the track gates dramatically oppose the otherwise rigidly straight lines of the design.

124. Oxner's IGA Foodliner (1958), 509–517 3rd Avenue West, Lunenburg, Nova Scotia (Rodney Construction Company) (above)   Here, form has been reduced to its essence – a rectangular box that shelters an activity. The provision of a large open area at a relatively low cost made this a popular model for commercial buildings across the country.

125. The Toronto-Dominion Centre (1964–71), Bay Street, Toronto, Ontario (Mies Van der Rohe and John Parkin, architects, with Bregman and Hamann) (facing page)   Set on an open plaza, the tall, steel-and-glass towers of the Toronto-Dominion Centre are classic examples of the International style skyscrapers as popularized by architect Mies Van der Rohe. The repetition of this formula in cities world-wide illustrates how truly international this style became.

126. 3188 Stanley Street, North Vancouver, British Columbia (above)
This modest home shows the influence of the International style on non-monumental structures. Strip windows and an open-grid canopy are combined with traditional clapboarding in a successful translation of originally steel- and concrete-based motifs to more typically Canadian wood construction.

The Brutalist Style

Brutalist architecture rejects the light, insubstantial quality of the International style in favour of weightier, monolithic masonry forms. While the International style explored the diaphanous aesthetic of glass and steel, Brutalism examines the beauty and power of concrete. Often, walls are constructed of load-bearing concrete; texture plays an important part in these surfaces and exaggerates the sense of mass. The surface of the concrete is often left with the patterns of the wooden mold, expressing the appeal of less highly machined finishes. Walls are sometimes faced with brick. In some cases, the fundamentalist qualities of Brutalism are expressed by placing the heating, plumbing, and electrical systems in ductwork on the exterior of the building. The rugged surfaces of these buildings are punctured by very few windows, which are often sealed, further accentuating the sense of an enclosed, protective environment. Although the name for this style may have originated from the French term for raw concrete, *béton brut*, it has been commonly accepted as descriptive of these buildings. The plans are complex and are expressed on the exterior in irregular, juxtaposed masses. In Canada the style often influenced the design of civic complexes whose large scale was appropriately expressed in massive, irregular profiles constructed of raw concrete. Variations on this theme include buildings with more highly finished surfaces and expressive shapes, some of which include symbolic content.

The Brutalist style redresses the lack of human warmth and variety of the glass-and-steel, "less is more" aesthetic. Just as Internationalism grew out of the need to rebuild Europe after the First World War, Brutalism was a response to new construction needs after the Second World War. In 1956, English architects Peter and Alison Smithson and Dutch architect Aldo van Eyck challenged the Internationalist ideology at the tenth meeting of the *Congrès Internationaux d'Architecture Moderne* (CIAM). Calling themselves "Team Ten," these architects took much of their inspiration from more utilitarian structures such as late-nineteenth-century warehouses and from earlier Expressionist architects such as Eric Mendelsohn (1887–1953; see *Expressionist Style*). In Britain the style was popular for public housing complexes and schools. Later the group developed into two related but distinct movements known as Structuralism and Brutalism.

127. National Arts Centre (1964–69), Elgin Street, Ottawa, Ontario (Affleck, Desbarats, Dimakopoulos, Lebensold and Sise, architects) (above) This large centre for the performing arts responds to its irregularly shaped site by using a series of triangles and hexagons as the basis of its plan. The juxtaposition of block-like masses, the textured surfaces, and the minimal fenestration create an enclosed, fortified impression, while allowing a tremendous freedom for internal planning; the complex includes theatres, exhibition and meeting spaces, restaurants, and offices.

128. School of Architecture (1969), Carleton University, Ottawa, Ontario (J. Stinson and C. Corneil, architects) (above)   This building owes as much to the ideas of the Dutch Structuralists as it does to Brutalism. Architects Jeff Stinson and Carmen Corneil claim to have been inspired by the 1920s Terminal Warehouse on Toronto's waterfront. The School of Architecture retains a clear suggestion of post and lintel construction while abandoning the highly machined finishes typical of Internationalism; instead, the architects have used construction materials more typical of industrial buildings. The unfinished look reflects the architects' belief that the building should allow its users to adapt its flexible spaces to their own needs.

129. Manitoba Theatre Centre (1969–70), 174 Market Street, Winnipeg, Manitoba (Number Ten Architectural Group) (above) During the late 1960s and early 1970s, scores of civic and performing arts centres were built across Canada in the Brutalist style. That style allowed flexibility in plans, to accommodate several different activities; the use of concrete was a cost-effective construction material; and the penchant for large areas of wall with minimal fenestration was well suited to the needs of theatres. This relatively modest theatre centre shows the influence of Dutch Structuralism in its unpretentious façade.

130. Grande Théâtre de Québec (1964–70), Quebec City, Quebec (V. Prus, architect) (facing page) The complex massing and concrete construction material of this centre for the performing arts are typical of Brutalist architecture in Canada. The building accommodates several theatres and performing spaces, as well as the necessary offices and public foyers.

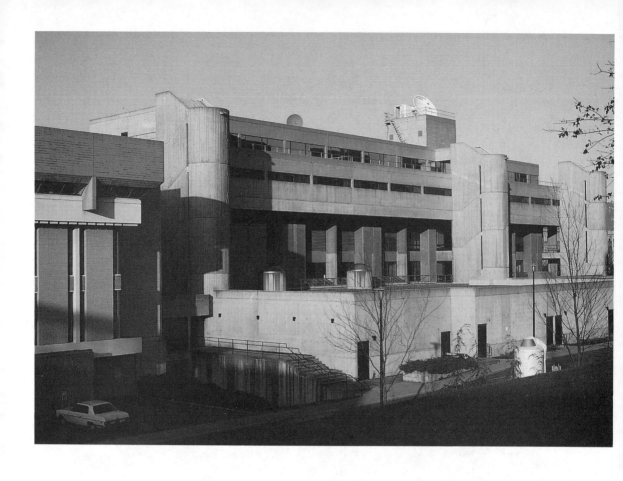

131. Medical Centre (1964; expanded 1970), University of British Columbia, Vancouver, British Columbia (Thompson, Berwick and Pratt, with McCarter, Nairn and Partners, architects) (above)
Originally built in 1964 in the International style, this building was expanded in 1970 with Brutalist themes such as the combination of brightly coloured metal piers and raw concrete walls; these features add warmth and boldly advertise the use of non-traditional materials. The complex massing with strong horizontals opposed by cylindrical stair towers not only satisfies a need for balance and diversity in the design, but also guides the viewer in understanding the building's plan.

132. Charlottetown Confederation Centre (1964), Charlottetown, Prince Edward Island (D. Dimak-opoulos, architect) (above)   This arts centre includes an art gallery, museum, memorial hall, theatre, and restaurant. It is a grouping of three distinct buildings lit by skylights and connected by underground walkways, a configuration typical of Brutalist planning and popular in Canada's cold, windswept winter cities. In deference to the Centre's siting near the historically important 1847 Province Building, the above-ground scale of the centre was minimized and its reinforced concrete frame was faced with Wallace sandstone.

The Expressionist Style

Expressionism is another approach to modern architecture. Popular in Canada from the 1960s through the 1970s, it rejects the sometimes rigid grid of Internationalism in order to exploit the sculptural and expressive possibilities of new construction techniques. Typical of Expressionist architecture are dramatically curved concrete or brick walls, cantilevered roofs, and the use of laminated wood in idiosyncratic shapes. This style has its roots in the European Expressionist movement of the early twentieth century. At that time, architects like Antonio Gaudí (1852–1926), Hans Poelzig (1869–1936) and Eric Mendelsohn (1887–1953) were experimenting with the ability of new materials, especially concrete, to produce dramatic and often eccentric structures. These early efforts were interrupted by the Second World War but presaged later designs by Le Corbusier (1887–1966), Eero Saarinen (1910–1961), and Alvar Aalto (1898–1976). The works of these Europeans, as well as the ground-breaking architecture of American Frank Lloyd Wright, inspired Canadian architects of the postwar period.

In Canada, the freedom of expression made possible by this approach to design allowed architects to relate their designs to the drama of our geography and climate as well as to incorporate specific cultural values. The liberation of design from supposedly universal values inspired architects throughout North and South America who were seeking to push design beyond its Euro-centric limitations. This empowered Indian, Métis, and other architects to infuse their designs with the cultural norms of their own communities. Since this style shares with Brutalism an emphasis on structural engineering and a similar handling of materials, some buildings exhibit qualities of both styles.

133. Arctic Research Laboratory (1973), Igloolik, Northwest Territories (Papineau, Gérin-Lajoie, Le-Blanc, Edwards [PGL Architects]) (facing page, top) This mushroom-shaped structure takes its inspiration from the Inuit igloo. Like the igloo, the main level is a single room. Laboratory units are arranged around the periphery. A high-tech version of vernacular form, the structure is built of a steel skeleton on a concrete substructure and is clad in fibre-glass reinforced plastic. Components were prefabricated in the south and erected on site by an Inuit construction team.

134. Heating and Cooling Plant, University of Regina (1967), Regina, Saskatchewan (Clifford Weins, architect) (facing page bottom) Clifford Weins captures the feel of the open prairies in the strong, sweeping shapes of this building. The fact that its shape derives solely from its structural system — pre-cast concrete A-frame units — illustrates the emphasis on structural engineering that is typical of many Expressionist style buildings.

135. Saint Mary's Church (1968), Red Deer, Alberta (Douglas J. Cardinal, architect) (above)
This stunning church rises like a sculpture from its flat, suburban setting. Cardinal combines Indian and European sensibilities in a plan recalling Le Corbusier's church of Notre-Dame du Haut at Ronchamp, France, while designing the curvilinear brick walls to echo natural forms. Structural sophistication was made possible by an early use of computer-assisted design. The tent-like roof is a canopy suspended on pre-tensioned cables from a supporting ring-beam.

136. Toronto City Hall (1965), Toronto, Ontario (Viljo Revell with John B. Parkin Associates, architects) (above)   The dramatic new city hall captures the monumental possibilities of the Expressionist style. The circular council chamber is symbolically supported and sheltered by the office blocks that curve protectively around it. This relatively restrained design illustrates the more rationalist approach to Expressionism.

137. Simon Fraser University (1965), South Burnaby, British Columbia (Erickson and Massey, architects, with Zoltan S. Kiss, Robert Harrison, Rhone and Iredale, and Duncan McNab, Harry Lee, and David Logan) (above) Sited just below the peak of Burnaby Mountain, this dramatic campus is referred to by its designer Arthur Erickson as "an Acropolis of our time." The plan is based on the idea of the inter-relationship of academic faculties and consists of four main components — the quadrangle, the library, the theatre and gymnasium, and the science block — that are connected by a skeleton of walkways. The heart of the complex is a three-storey central mall covered by a glazed roof constructed of laminated fir beams tensioned by steel tie-rods.

138. Notre Dame des Champs (1963), Repentigny, Quebec (Roger d'Astous, architect) (above)
The 1960s saw the construction of a number of Roman Catholic churches in Quebec that broke with the traditional, twin-tower design. Roger d'Astous's design at Notre Dame des Champs breaks up the church into separate volumes — an open-frame bell-tower, a sheltering marquee, a vaulted entry vestibule, and the soaring body of the church proper. In his use of these futuristic shapes he may have been influenced by the teachings of Frank Lloyd Wright, under whom d'Astous studied.

The Post-Modern Style

Post-Modern architects reject the Internationalists' belief in absolute ideals and formal perfection. There are, therefore, no rules in Post-Modernism. Running counter to the ahistorical tendencies of much of late-twentieth-century architecture, it is an eclectic style that regards all of architectural history as fair game. Typically, Post-Modernism reinstates the principal façade as the focus of the design, using a decorated main entry as the central element, and further elaborates the building with complex roof shapes, applied ornament, and vibrantly coloured surfaces. Look for architectural motifs used in inventive and imaginative ways, ways that defy conventional rules: classical columns that offer no support, for instance. The choice of materials and motifs often draws upon the local context, in an attempt to be more sensitive to vernacular traditions and regional culture. Post-Modernism restores the qualities of individuality, novelty, and even humour to our built environment.

Post-Modernism has been influenced by a number of architects, such as Robert Venturi, Frank Gehry, and Robert Graves. To some extent, they all parody the earnestness of former architectural movements. Venturi, for example, defends the value of American twentieth-century vernacular architecture of the drive-in restaurant and Las Vegas "strip" type; Gehry produces deconstructed houses whose fractured forms play with the normally sacrosant organization of space; and Graves invents historicist images, often based on neoclassical precedents. In Canada, Post-Modern architecture has resulted in an increase in the variety of architectural motifs used in large, commercial, or civic complexes. In house design, Post-Modernism has offered a revival of certain vernacular forms, particularly those based upon classical design.

139. Portage Place (1985–87), North Portage Avenue, Winnipeg, Manitoba (RTKL Architects, Number Ten Architectural Group, Smith Carter Architects, IKOY Partnership, Austin Company, Webb Zerafa, Stechesen Katz, and Cockburn McFeetors) (above) The involvement of a large team of architects, engineers, and builders is now common in large-scale contemporary architectural projects. The design plays with the image of the vernacular pitched roof but is executed in slick steel and glass materials, a typically Post-Modern reinterpretation of old forms in new ways.

140. 140a. Mississauga City Hall (1982–87), Mississauga, Ontario (E. Jones and M. Kirkland, architects) (above and facing page) The Mississauga City Hall complex is one of the boldest expressions of Post-Modernism in Canada. The juxtaposition of simple, geometrical shapes and the reinterpretation of familiar building types, such as the gable-fronted structure and the rectangular commercial block, lend this complex a futuristic air despite its use of historical models. The buildings have been compared variously to neoclassical prototypes and to a cluster of Ontario farm buildings (the clock tower as windmill, the pitched-roofed building as barn, the office building as farm house, and the cylindrical council chamber as silo).

**141. National Gallery of Canada (1983–88), Sussex Drive, Ottawa, Ontario (Moshe Safdie, architect)
(above)**   The gallery is a massive structure whose main façade is hidden behind a sophisticated glass cage, which mirrors the shapes of the Parliament Buildings nearby. Despite Safdie's denial of Post-Modernism, his use of concrete and glass to reinterpret older masonry forms is typical of the style's sensitivity to context.

142. House, West 2nd Avenue, Vancouver, British Columbia (above)
A typical, vernacular type for Vancouver, this house has been given a face-lift. The new façade is set visibly apart from the house proper, so that there is no question which is which. The fragmentation of a building's component parts is a favourite technique of Post-Modern architects.

143. Bradley House (1977), North Hatley, Quebec (Peter Rose, architect) (above)
This house mixes a variety of familiar vernacular shapes, such as pitched roofs and gable windows, with Gothic-arched windows, in a whimsical amalgam. The use of traditional wood sheathing adds to its folksy charm and attempts to relate the structure to its setting.

Glossary

This is a list of definitions of architectural terms that appear in the text. For more expansive definitions, consult: Cyril M. Harris, ed., *Illustrated Dictionary of Historic Architecture* (New York: Dover, 1977).

Acanthus leaf: Stylized mediterranean leaf form used as decoration especially for the capitals of Corinthian and Composite orders.

Applied order: see order.

Apse: a semicircular or vaulted end to a church.

Arcade: a series of arches on columns or piers supporting a wall.

Arcuated construction: construction that is, or appears to be, based upon arches for support.

Bakelite: an insulating or facing material manufactured from synthetic resins and resembling opaque glass.

Balustrade: a low rail supported by short posts.

Bay: the vertical divisions in a façade created by the rhythm of the doors and windows.

Bellcast roof: a roof that flares out at the eaves.

Belvedere: an enclosed structure on the roof intended as a look-out.

Blind arcade: a row of arches applied to a wall as a decorative element.

Board and batten: wooden sheathing of wide vertical boards placed side by side with narrow strips of wood (called battens) covering the joints.

Bracket: a small projecting piece of stone or wood that supports a horizontal member such as the eaves.

Bull's eye window: a round window; also called an oculus.

Buttress: an exterior masonry support built into or against a wall to counter the lateral thrusts of a roof.

Cantilever: a horizontal projection balanced by the downward pressure of a vertical member on its pivotal point.

Casement window: a window that is hinged along the vertical edge and opens by swinging either in or out.

Chancel: the part of a church to the liturgical east of the nave or crossing containing the altar; also known as the sanctuary.

Clocher: bell tower or a room near the top of a tower where the bells are hung.

Colonette: a small decorative column.

Colonnade: a row of regularly spaced columns usually supporting an entablature and part of a roof.

Column: a tall, cylindrical support, traditionally decorated according to one of the ancient orders (see order).

Console: an S-curve bracket.

Corbel: a block that projects to support a horizontal member, usually the eaves.

Cornice: a projecting moulding that crowns the top of a building; it also forms the upper part of an entablature.

Crenellation: a regular series of gaps in the parapet or low wall running along the top of a wall.

Cresting: ornamental decoration along the roofline, usually made of iron.

Crocket: a decorative roof ornament, usually in leaf shape, commonly found in Gothic Revival architecture.

Cross window: a window whose mullion and transom cross, forming four lights and a cross shape.

Cupola: a small dome.

Dentil: a small block, usually part of a series of such blocks, in the entablature of the classical orders (see order).

Doric: see order.

Drip mouldings: a moulding over a door or window that casts off rain.

Ecclesiology: the study of the building, style, and arrangement of churches, particularly nineteenth-century Gothic churches.

Elevation: the face of a building; an architectural drawing of the vertical projection of the face of a building.

English baroque: English classical architecture of the seventeenth and early eighteenth centuries.

Entablature: the upper horizontal bar or beam, resting on the capitals of a classical order, whose parts consist of a cornice, frieze, and architrave.

Earred trim: a moulding that frames the top and upper part of a window or door terminating in a short projection.

Fanlight: a small semicircular or elliptical window above a door with radiating bars, resembling a fan.

Fenestration: the arrangement of windows on a building.

Finial: an ornament at the top of a gable or roofline.

Frieze: a wide band at the top of the order (see order), between the architrave and the cornice.

Frontispiece: an ornamental porch.

Gambrel: a ridged roof with two slopes on each side.

Giant order: an order that rises the full height of the façade (see order).

Gibbs surround: the surround of a door or window that is composed of alternating large and small blocks of stone.

Glazing bars: the small members that hold the glass in place in a window.

Half-timbering: exposed imitation timber-framing in which the spaces between the frame are filled with rubble or brick and may be painted or plastered.

Hipped roof: roof with four pitched sides.

Hood moulding: a moulding that projects above a window or door to throw off rainwater.

Ionic: see order.

Key pattern: ornamental design or fretwork of interlacing right-angled lines in contrasting patterns of light and dark.

Keystone: the central stone at the apex of an arch of vault.

Label moulding: a square-arched moulding that runs along the top and part way down a window or door.

Lancet: Gothic narrow pointed window, used mainly in churches.

Lintel: a horizontal beam above a window or door that takes the weight of the wall above the opening.

Longhouse: a long structure built of bent poles forming a tunnel shape, capable of housing several families.

Mullion: a vertical member in a window that subdivides the window into two or more lights.

Niche: a concave recess in a wall, often intended to contain sculpture.

Oculus: a round or oval opening in a wall or at the apex of a dome; sometimes louvred or glazed; also called a roundel or bull's eye window.

Ogee: an arch created from a double curve, convex above and concave below.

Order: an arrangement of columns and entablature in classical architecture. Specific styles of columns and detailing are divided into five main categories: Doric, Ionic, Corinthian (the Greek orders), Tuscan, and Composite (the Roman orders).

Oriel: a bay window projecting from an upper storey.

Palladian window: a three-part window consisting of a tall centre window, usually round-headed, flanked by two shorter, narrower windows.

Parapet: a low wall at the edge of a roof or balcony.

Pavilion: a subsection of a larger building, usually projecting, sometimes distinguished by a different roof shape or surface treatment, usually at the centre or ends of a building.

Pediment: the triangular gable end of a roof usually over an entrance or window, sometimes decorated with sculpture; variations of the simple triangular form include curved sides or sides broken off at the apex.

Pier: a vertical stone or brick support, usually square or rectangular.

Pilaster: a pillar or pier attached to a wall, usually in one of the classical orders.

Plinth: the base of a column, pilaster, door frame, or wall resembling a platform.

Portico: a covered porch or walkway supported by columns.

Quoin: a protruding stone or brick that accentuates an exterior corner.

Reinforced concrete: concrete strengthened by the addition of at least 0.2 per cent structural steel.

Rose window: a large circular window with radiating tracery or glazing bars; often filled with stained glass.

Rosette: a round motif applied to a wall, or as a centre ceiling decoration, usually decorated with floral or leaf motifs.

Rustication: cut stone with textured block faces.

Sidelight: a window beside a door, often in flanking pairs.

Sill: the horizontal piece at the bottom of a window frame; the bottom of the door frame resting on the foundation.

Speed-stripes: horizontal decorative stripes applied to Moderne and Art Deco designs to emphasize the aerodynamic shapes and heighten the sensation of movement and speed.

Stringcourse: a protruding band that runs horizontally along the façade of a building, usually between storeys.

Structural steel frame: a building system in which steel members such as girders and beams support the weight of the building.

Terrazzo: flooring manufactured from marble chips irregularly set in cement and highly polished.

Tourelle: a turret or small round tower projecting from the upper corner of a wall.

Transom: strictly, refers to a horizontal bar over a window or door, but often used to describe a window above a transom bar.

Trefoil: a three-lobed cloverleaf pattern.

Tudor arch: a shallow pointed arch (a four-centred arch).

Vault: a covering over an arched area. Various shapes include: barrel vault, which is a semicircular or barrel shape; fan vault, a Gothic-style vault in a concave conical shape; rib vault, a vault in which the ribs support the web between.

Vernacular building: building not designed by a professional architect and usually deriving its form and materials from local or inherited tradition.

Voussoirs: wedge-shaped stones or bricks set in an arch, often over a window or doorway.

Ziggurat: refers to the shape of stepped-back skyscrapers and derives from Mesopotamian and pre-Columbian temples, which rose in stages of successively diminishing size.

Suggested Reading

This is a partial list of principal Canadian secondary sources. The titles listed offer good, general coverage of certain areas of interest. Local histories and guide books, journal and magazine articles, information on individual buildings, exhibition catalogues, bibliographies, and good secondary sources on related topics for American and European architecture are too numerous to mention here. For further information on any topic of interest, consult your librarian. Especially useful is Geoffrey Simmons, comp., *Bibliography of Canadian Architecture/Bibliographie d'architecture canadienne* Ottawa: Society for the Study of Architecture in Canada, 1992.

Archibald, Margaret. *By Federal Design: The Chief Architect's Branch of the Department of Public Works, 1881–1914* Ottawa: Parks Canada, 1983.

Ball, Norman, ed. *Building Canada: A History of Public Works.* Toronto: University of Toronto Press, 1988.

Barrett, Anthony, A., and Rhodri W. Liscombe. *Francis Rattenbury and British Columbia: Architecture and Challenge in the Imperial Age.* Vancouver: University of British Columbia, 1983.

Beckman, Margaret, Stephen Langmead, and John Black. *The Best Gift: A Record of the Carnegie Libraries in Ontario.* Toronto: Dundurn, 1984.

Bergeron, Claude. *Architectures du XXe siècle au Québec*. Montreal: Éditions du Méridien, 1989.

——. *L'architecture des églises au Québec, 1940–1985*. Quebec: Laval University Press, 1987.

Bergevin, Hélène. *Églises Protestants*. Montreal: Libre Expression, 1981.

Bingham, Janet. *Samuel Maclure: Architect*. Ganges, B.C.: Horsdal and Schubart, 1985.

Bland, John, et al. *The Architecture of Edward and W.S. Maxwell*. Montreal: Museum of Fine Arts, 1991.

Blumenson, John. *Ontario Architecture*. Markham: Fitzhenry and Whiteside, 1990.

Boddy, Trevor. *The Architecture of Douglas Cardinal*. Edmonton: NeWest, 1989.

——. *Modern Architecture in Alberta*. Edmonton: Alberta Culture and Multiculturalism and The Canadian Plains Research Centre, 1987.

Brooks, H. Allen. *The Prairie School: Frank Lloyd Wright and his midwest contemporaries*. Toronto: University of Toronto Press, 1972.

Brosseau, Mathilde. *Gothic Revival in Canadian Architecture*. Ottawa: Parks Canada, 1980.

Brown, Ron. *The Train Doesn't Stop Here Anymore.: An Illustrated History of Railway Stations in Canada*. Peterborough: Broadview, 1991.

Cameron, Christina. *Charles Baillairgé, Architect, Engineer*. Montreal: McGill-Queen's University Press, 1989.

Cameron, Christina, and Monique Trépanier. *Vieux Québec: son architecture intérieure*. Ottawa: National Museum of Man, 1986.

Cameron, Christina, and Janet Wright. *Second Empire Style in Canadian Architecture*. Ottawa: Parks Canada, 1980.

Carroll, Jacqueline. *Muskoka Boathouses*. Erin, Ont: Boston Mills, 1990.

Carter, Margaret, comp. *Early Canadian Court Houses*. Ottawa: Parks Canada, 1983.

Cawker, Ruth. *Viewpoints: One Hundred Years of Architecture in Ontario, 1889–1989.* Toronto: Ontario Association of Architects, 1989.

Cawker, Ruth, and William Bernstein. *Contemporary Canadian Architecture: The Mainstream and Beyond.* Markham: Fitzhenry and Whiteside, 1982.

——, comps. *Building with Words: Canadian Architects on Architecture.* Toronto: Coach House, 1981.

Chalmers, Graeme, and Frances Moorcroft. *British Columbia Houses: Guide to the Styles of Domestic Architecture in British Columbia.* Vancouver: Wedge, 1981.

Clerk, Nathalie. *Palladian Style in Canadian Architecture.* Ottawa: Parks Canada, 1984.

——. *Le Style Beaux-Arts au Canada.* Ottawa: Canadian Parks Service, forthcoming.

Crossman, Kelly. *Architecture in Transition: From Art to Practice, 1885–1906.* Montreal: McGill-Queen's University Press, 1987.

Dangelmaier, Rudi. *Pioneer Buildings of British Columbia.* Madeira Park, B.C.: Harbour, 1989.

de Caraffe, Marc, C.A. Hale, Dana Johnson, G.E. Mills, and Margaret Carter. *Town Halls of Canada.* Ottawa: Parks Canada, 1987.

Dennis, Thelma B. *Albertans Built: Aspects of Housing in Rural Alberta to 1920.* Edmonton: University of Alberta, 1986.

Downs, Barry. *Sacred Places: British Columbia's Early Churches.* Vancouver: Douglas and McIntyre, 1980.

Duffus, Allan, Edward MacFarlane, Elizabeth Pacey and George Rogers. *Thy Dwellings Fair: Churches of Nova Scotia 1750–1830.* Hantsport, N.S.: Lancelot, 1982.

Erickson, Arthur. *The Architecture of Arthur Erickson.* Vancouver: Douglas and McIntyre, 1988.

Freedman, Adele. *Sight Lines: Looking at Architecture and Design in Canada.* Don Mills: Oxford University Press, 1990.

Gagnon-Pratte, France. *Country Houses for Montrealers, 1892–1924: The Architecture of E. and W.S. Maxwell.* Montreal: Meridian, 1987.

Gauthier, Raymonde. *Les manoirs du Québec*. Québec: Fides, 1976.

——. *La tradition en architecture québécoise: Le XXe siècle*. Montreal: Éditions du Méridien, 1989.

Fournay, Isabelle, ed. *Ernest Cormier and the Université de Montréal*. Montreal: Canadian Centre for Architecture, 1990.

Gowans, Alan. *The Comfortable House: North American Suburban Architecture, 1890–1930*. Cambridge: MIT Press, 1986

——. *Looking at Architecture in Canada*. Toronto: Oxford University Press, 1958.

(no author). *Historical Architecture of Saskatchewan*. Regina: Focus, 1986.

Hubbard, R.H. *Ample Mansions: the Viceregal Residences of the Canadian Provinces*. Ottawa: University of Ottawa Press, 1989.

Hunt, Geoffrey. *John M. Lyle: Toward a Canadian Architecture*. Kingston: Agnes Etherington Art Centre, 1982.

Kalman, Harold. *History of Canadian Architecture*. Don Mills, Ont.: Oxford University Press, forthcoming in 1993.

Kalman, Harold, and John de Visser. *Pioneer Churches*. Toronto: McClelland and Stewart, 1976.

Kalman, Harold, and Joan Mackie. *The Architecture of W.E. Noffke*. Ottawa: Heritage Ottawa, 1976.

Lamy, Laurent, and Jean-Claude Jurni. *Architecture contemporaine au Québec, 1960–1970*. Montreal: Éditions de l'Hexagone, 1983.

Lessard, Michel, and Huguette Marquis. *Encyclopédie de la maison québécoise: Trois siècles d'habitations*. Montréal: Les éditions de l'homme, 1972.

Levitt, Sheldon, Lynn Milstone, and Sidney T. Tenenbaum. *Treasures of a People: The Synagogues of Canada*. Toronto: Lester and Orpen Dennys, 1985.

MacRae, Marion. *The Ancestral Roof: Domestic Architecture of Upper Canada*. Toronto: Clarke, Irwin, 1963.

MacRae, Marion, and Anthony Adamson. *Cornerstones of Order: Courthouses and Town Halls of Ontario, 1784–1914.* Toronto: Osgoode Society, 1983.

———. *Hallowed Walls: Church Architecture of Upper Canada.* Toronto: Clarke, Irwin, 1970.

Maitland, Leslie. *Neoclassical Architecture in Canada.* Ottawa: Parks Canada, 1984.

———. *The Queen Anne Revival in Canadian Architecture.* Ottawa: Canadian Parks Service, 1990.

Martin, J. Edward. *The Railway Stations of Western Canada: An Architectural History.* White Rock, B.C.: Studio E, 1980.

Martin, Paul-Louis, and Jean Lavoie, ed. *Les chemins de la mémoire: Monuments et sites historiques du Québec.* Quebec: Publications du Québec, 1990–91.

Mika, Nick. *Historic Mills of Ontario.* Belleville: Mika Publishers, 1987.

Mills, G.E. *Buying Wood and Building Farms: Marketing Lumber and Farm Building Designs on the Canadian Prairies 1880–1920.* Ottawa: Parks Canada, 1991.

Moir, Gillian, Helen Orr, Ione Thorkelsson, Irene Kuziw, John Hockman. *Early Buildings of Manitoba.* Winnipeg: Peguis, 1973.

Moogk, Peter N. *Building a House in New France.* Toronto: McClelland and Stewart, 1977.

Nabokov, Peter, and Robert Eastman. *Native American Architecture.* New York: Oxford University Press, 1989.

Noppen, Luc. *Les églises du Québec 1600–1850.* Quebec: Editeur officiel du Québec, 1977.

Noppen, Luc, Claude Paulette and Michel Tremblay. *Québec: Trois siècles d'architecture.* Quebec: Libre Expression, 1979.

Ondaatje, Kim. *Small Churches of Canada.* Toronto: Lester and Orpen Dennys, 1982.

Pacey, Elizabeth, George Rogers and Allan Duffus. *More Stately Mansions: Churches of Nova Scotia 1830–1910.* Hantsport, N.S.: Lancelot, 1983.

Preyde, James, and Susan Preyde. *The Steeple Chase: Ontario's Historic Churches*. Erin, Ont.: Boston Mills, 1990.

Reksten, Terry. *Rattenbury*. Victoria: Sono Nis, 1978.

Remillard, François, and Brian Merrett. *Mansions of the Golden Square Mile, Montreal 1850–1930*. Montreal: Meridian, 1987.

Rempel, John I. *Building with Wood, and Other Aspects of Nineteenth Century Building in Central Canada*, rev. ed. Toronto: University of Toronto Press, 1980.

Richardson, A.J.H., Geneviève Bastien, Doris Dubé and Marthe Lacombe. *Québec City: Architects, Artisans and Builders*. Ottawa: National Museum of Man, 1984.

Scott Smith, H.M. *The Historic Churches of Prince Edward Island*. Erin, Ontario: Boston Mills Press, 1986.

——. *The Historic Houses of Prince Edward Island*. Erin, Ont.: Boston Mills, 1990.

Segger, Martin. *The Buildings of Samuel Maclure: In Search of Appropriate Form*. Victoria: Sono Nis, 1986.

Tuck, Robert C. *Gothic Dreams: The Life and Times of a Canadian Architect, William Critchlow Harris 1854–1913*. Toronto: Dundurn, 1978.

Veillette, John, and Gary White. *Early Indian Village Churches: Wooden Frontier Architecture in British Columbia*. Vancouver: University of British Columbia Press, 1977.

Wagg, Susan. *Percy Erskine Nobbs: Architect, Artist, Craftsman*. Kingston: McGill-Queen's University Press, 1982.

Wetherell, Donald G., and Irene R.A. Kmet. *Homes in Alberta: Building, Trends, and Design, 1870-1967*. Edmonton: University of Alberta, 1991.

Whiteson, Leon. *Modern Canadian Architecture*. Edmonton: Hurtig, 1983.

Woodall, Ronald, and T.H. Watkins. *Taken by the Wind: Vanishing Architecture of the West*. Don Mills, Ont.: General Publishing, 1977.

Photo Credits

Environment Canada, Canadian Inventory of Historic Building: 1, 2, 3, 10, 11, 17, 23, 25, 27, 28, 29, 32, 33, 38, 40, 41, 42, 43, 44, 48, 55, 56, 57, 58, 60, 65, 77, 79, 82, 111, 141

Public Works Canada, Heritage Recording Services: 4, 5, 6, 7, 8, 9, 12, 13, 14, 15, 16, 18, 19, 20, 21, 22, 26, 30, 31, 34, 35, 36, 39, 45, 46, 47, 49, 52, 53, 64, 66, 67, 69, 70, 71, 72, 73, 75, 76, 84, 89, 90, 91, 93, 94, 96, 99, 112

Environment Canada — Parks: 24

J. Hucker: 37, 59, 63, 115

Helmut Schade: front cover, 83, 87, 92, 105, 119, 121, 125, 126, 129, 130, 131, 132, 134, 135, 136, 137, 138, 142, 143

Monique Trépanier: 51, 54, 61, 80, 120

H. Scott Smith: 50

Saskatchewan Culture and Recreation: 62, 74, 78, 85, 86, 88, 103, 113, 114

Leslie Maitland: 68, 95, 97, 110, 122

Heritage Canada: 81, 100, 107, 118

Shannon Ricketts: 98

Tom Horrocks: 101, 124, 139, 140, 140a

Frank Haigh: 102, 104, 106, 109, 117, 123, 127, 128, rear cover

Communauté Urbain de Montréal: 108

Environment Canada, Photographic Services: 116

Harald Finkler: 133

Index

This is an index to building names, cities or towns, provinces or territories, and architects' names. References are to page numbers.

Admiralty House, Halifax, Nova Scotia 26
Affleck, Desbarats, Dimakopoulos, Lebensold and Sise 186
Alberta 31, 73, 91, 150, 177, 194
Alexandra Bar, Drumheller, Alberta 150
Alley, Thomas 63
Allward and Gouinlock 179
Amherst, Nova Scotia 79, 136
Angus McIntyre House, Montreal, Quebec 94
Archibald, John S. 96
Architecture, School of, Carleton University, Ottawa, Ont. 187
Arctic Research Laboratory, Igloolik, NWT 192
Atlantic Canada 13, 31, 33
Auburn, Nova Scotia 29
Austin Company 199

Baillif, Claude 18
Balfour Building, Toronto, Ont. 146

Barkerville, B.C. 55
Barott, Ernest I. 137
Bank of Montreal, Ottawa, Ont. 137
Bank of Nova Scotia, Halifax, N.S. 146
Belleville, Ontario 60
Bellevue House, Kingston, Ontario 60
Berlinguet, François-Xavier 73, 76, 116
Berwick (Thompson, Berkwick and Pratt) 190
Bessborough Armoury, Vancouver, B.C. 145
Bessborough Hotel, Saskatoon, Sask. 96
Birkbeck Building, Toronto, Ont. 121
Blackmore 92
Blackstone 92
Blair, William Wallace 102
Booth House, Ottawa, Ont. 164
Bradley House, North Hatley, Que. 204
Bregman and Hamann 182
British Columbia 16, 31, 33, 55, 83, 96, 100, 105, 125, 134, 140, 145, 156, 158, 164, 184, 190, 196, 203

Brock House, Vancouver, B.C. 156
Brown, Benjamin 146
Brown and Vallance 168
Browne, George 36, 42, 60
Burke and Horwood 100
Burton, H. (Pope and) 177

Canada Building, Saskatoon, Sask. 130
Canadian Imperial Bank of Commerce, Dawson, Yukon 115
Canadian Imperial Bank of Commerce, Watson, Sask. 116
Capitol Theatre, Prince Rupert, B.C. 158
Cardinal, Douglas J. 194
Cardston, Alta 91, 177
Cardston Court House, Cardston, Alta. 91
Carleton University, Ottawa, Ontario 187
Caserne No. 1, Montreal, Que. 176
Centre Block, Ottawa, Ont. 171
Charlottetown, P.E.I. 63, 76, 103, 191
Charlottetown Confederation Centre, Charlottetown, P.E.I. 191
Château Dufresne, Montreal, Que. 114
Château Frontenac, Quebec City, Que. 93
Château Laurier, Ottawa, Ont. 93, 94
Château St. Louis, Quebec City, Que. 12
Child's Building, Winnipeg, Man. 118
Chisholm, James and Sons 130
Christ Church Anglican Cathedral, Fredericton, NB.52
Church of Jesus Christ of the Latter Day Saints, Cardston, Alta. 177
City Delivery Building, Toronto, Ont. 142
City Hall, Guelph, Ont. 60
City Hall, Vancouver, B.C. 134
Cockburn McFeeters 199
Colonial Building, St. John's, Nfld. 36
Confederation Building, Winnipeg, Man. 128
Connolly, Joseph 73
Coombs English Shoe Store (Former), Halifax, NS. 63
Cormier, Ernest 145
Cormier House, Montreal, Que. 145
Corneil, C. (Stinson and) 187
Cumberland, Frederick 81, 85
Cunningham, John 47, 48
Cutler, Manley N. 73

Daly Building, Ottawa, Ont. 124, 128
Darling and Pearson 116, 125
d'Astous, Roger 197
Dawson, Yukon 50, 115
de Poitras, Martin 86
Desbarats (of Affleck, Desbarats, Dimakopoulos, Lebensold and Sise) 186
Dimakopoulos (of Affleck, Desbarats, Dimakopoulos, Lebensold and Sise) 186
Dimakopoulos, D. 191
Dodd, W., and Co., 158
Dolphin, Charles B. 142
Dorval, Que. 162
Drumheller, Alta. 150
Du Calvet House, Montreal, Que. 16
Dufresne and Renard 114
Dufresne, Marius 176
Dundas Terrace, Charlottetown, P.E.I. 103

Earle, Stephen C. 57
Edey, Moses C. 128
Edwards (of Papineau, Gerin-Lajoie, LeBlanc, Edwards) 192
Erickson and Massey 196
Ewart, John 47

Fairn, Leslie R. 136
Federal Building, Amherst, N.S. 136
Federal Building, Regina, Sask. 135
Fellheimer and Wagner 149
Fire Station No. 10 (Former), Ottawa, Ont. 160
Fort Saint James, B.C. 16
Fox (Maclure and) 156
Fredericton, N.B. 24, 52
Fuller, Thomas 78, 79

Garage Roadhouse, Wolfville, N.S. 150
Gardiner, Mercer and Gardiner 125
Gérin-Lajoie (of Papineau, Gérin-Lajoie, LeBlanc, Edwards) 192
Gouinlock, George W. 121
Gouinlock (Allward and) 179

Government House (Former), Federicton, N.B. 24
Grande Allée Drill Hall, Quebec City, Que. 93, 94
Grande Théâtre de Quebec, Quebec City, Que.
  188
Gray, J. Wilson 128
Guelph, Ont. 60, 73

Halifax, N.S. 26, 41, 63, 146
Hall, Captain 22
Hamann (Bregman and) 182
Hamilton, Ont. 55, 149
Hammond, William G. 40
Hammond Residence, Sackville, N.B. 100
Hargreaves, H., and N.L. Thompson 174
Harris, William Critchlow 81, 103
Harrison, Robert 196
Hart House, Toronto, Ont. 167
Heating and Cooling Plant, University of Regina,
  Regina, Sask. 192
Holoston, B., and Jim Parsons 150
Holy Trinity Anglican Cathedral, Quebec City,
  Que. 22
Hooper Residence Victoria, B.C. 100
Hooper, Thomas 100
Hooper and Watkins 105
Horticulture Building, Ottawa, Ont. 175
Horwood (Burke and) 100
Hunter, J.M. 76
Hunting House, Vancouver, B.C. 164
Hyde (Nobbs and) 162

Igloolik, N.W.T. 192
IKOY Partnership 199
Iredale (Rhone and) 196

Jesuit Seminary, Quebec City, Que. 12
Jones (Fuller and) 78
Jones, E., and M. Kirkland 200
Jones, H.G. 112

Katz (Stechesen Katz) 199
Kingston, Ont. 36, 42, 60
Kirkland, M. (Jones and Kirkland)~200

Kiss, Zoltan S. 196
Kough, Patrick 36

Laurentian Club, Ottawa, Ont. 100
Law Courts, Charlottetown, P.E.I. 63
Lebensold (of Affleck, Desbarats, Dimakopoulos,
  Lebensold and Sise) 186
Leblanc, Augustin 38
LeBlanc (of Papineau, Gérin-Lajoie, LeBlanc,
  Edwards) 192
Lee, Harry 196
Lemay, R.P. 116
Lennox, Edward James 90
Library of Parliament, Ottawa, Ontario 78
Liverpool, N.S. 40
Lockport, Man. 49
Logan, David 196
London, Ont. 47
Lunenburg, N.S. 182
Lyle, John M. 112, 146
Lyon Building, Winnipeg, Manitoba 92

Macdonald Engineering Building, Toronto,
  Ont. 123
Macdonald (Ross and) 112
MacFarlane (Ross and) 94
MacLaren, J.P. 163
Maclure and Fox 156
Maison du jardinier, Dorval, Que. 162
Manitoba 31, 49, 92, 102, 118, 125, 128, 188,
  199
Manitoba Theatre Centre, Winnipeg, Man. 188
Marchand, J.O., (J.A. Pearson and) 171
Marine Building, Vancouver, B.C. 140
Maritimes 15
Martin 86
Massey (Erickson and) 196
Masson, G., (H. Sheppard and) 150
Matheson and Townley 134
Matthews, W. 29
Mauvide-Genest (Manoir), Saint Jean, Que. 18
Maxwell, Edward 88, 94
Maxwell, E., and W.S. 121
McCallum Building, Regina, Saskatchewan 130
McCarter and Nairne 140, 190

McFeeters (Cockburn and) 199
McGill University, Montreal, Que. 123
McNabb, Duncan 196
Mechanical Engineering Building, Toronto, Ont. 179
Medical Centre, University of British Columbia, Vancouver, B.C. 190
Medicine Hat, Alta. 73
Melville, Saskatchewan 138
Mercer (Gardiner, Mercer and Gardiner) 125
Mesnard, Albert 83
Mill Restaurant, Ottawa, Ont. 29
Middlesex County Court House, London, Ont. 47
Mississauga City Hall, Mississauga, Ont. 200
Mississauga, Ont. 200
Montreal, Que. 12, 13, 16, 44, 83, 86, 88, 94, 109, 114, 123, 145, 170, 176
Montreal Diocesan Theological College, Montreal, Que. 83
Moose Jaw, Saskatchewan 123, 168, 174

Nairne (McCarter and) 140, 190
Natatorium, Moose Jaw, Sask. 174
National Arts Centre, Ottawa, Ont. 186
National Gallery of Art, Ottawa, Ont. 202
New Brunswick 13, 24, 47, 48, 52, 100
New Westminster, B.C. 125
Newfoundland 36, 57, 86
Nicolet, Que. 38
Nobbs, P.E. 123
Nobbs and Hyde 162
Noffke, W.E. 154, 156, 160
North Hatley, Que. 204
North Vancouver, B.C. 184
Northwest Territories 192
North-west Territories 31
Notre Dame, Montreal, Que. 44
Notre Dame-des-Champs, Repentigny, Que. 197
Notre Dame-des-Victoires, Quebec City, Que. 18
Notre Dame-du-Sacre-Coeur, Quebec City, Que. 73
Nova Scotia 13, 26, 29, 40, 41, 63, 79, 136, 146, 150, 182
Number Ten Architectural Group 188, 199

O'Donnell, James 44

Ontario 13, 15, 29, 31, 36, 42, 47, 55, 57, 60, 73, 78, 81, 85, 90, 94, 100, 107, 112, 121, 124, 128, 137, 142, 146, 149, 150, 154, 156, 160, 163, 164, 167, 171, 173, 175, 179, 180, 182, 186, 187, 195, 200, 202
Ottawa, Ont. 29, 78, 93, 94, 100, 124, 128, 137, 154, 156, 160, 163, 164, 171, 172, 173, 175, 186, 187, 202
Our Lady of the Immaculate Conception, Guelph, Ont. 73
Oxner's IGA Foodliner, Lunenburg, N.S. 182

Painter, Walter S. 88, 116
Papineau, Gérin-Lajoie, LeBlanc, Edwards 192
Parkin, J.B., and Associates 180, 182, 195
Parliament, Ottawa, Ont. 171
Parsons, Jim (B. Holoston and) 150
Pearson (Darling and) 116, 125
Pearson, J.A., and J.O. Marchand 171
Perrault, Maurice 83
Perry, R.T. 145
PGL Architects 192
Pope, H., and H. Burton 177
Portnall, (Reilly and) 135
Port Hope, Ont. 57
Portage Place, Winnipeg, Man. 199
Post Office, Amherst, N.S. 79
Post Office, Moose Jaw, Sask. 123
Pratt (Thompson, Berwick and Pratt) 190
Price, Bruce 88
Prince Edward Island 63, 73, 76, 81, 103, 191
Prince Rupert, Sask. 158
Provincial Court House, Weyburn, Sask. 155
Prus, V. 188

Quebec (province) 10, 12, 15, 16, 18, 20, 22, 26, 31, 33, 38, 44, 73, 83, 86, 88, 94, 109, 114, 116, 123, 145, 162, 170, 176, 188, 197, 204
Quebec City, Que. 12, 13, 18, 20, 22, 26, 38, 73, 93, 94, 116, 188
Queen's County Court House, Liverpool, N.S. 40

Red Deer, Alta. 194
Regina, Sask. 121, 130, 135, 192

Reilly and Portnall 135
Renard (Dufresne and) 114
Repentigny, Que. 197
Revell, Viljo 195
Rhone and Iredale 196
Rideau Branch Public Library, Ottawa, Ont. 163
Robe, Major 22
Robert Simpson Store, Toronto, Ont. 107, 124
Rockwood Villa, Kingston, Ont. 36
Rodney Construction Company 182
Roger's Chocolates, Victoria, B.C. 105
Rolph, Ernest, and Henry Sproatt 167
Rose, Peter 204
Roslyn Court Apartments, Winnipeg, Man. 102
Ross and Macdonald 112
Ross and MacFarlane 94
RTKL Architects 199
Russell, John H.G. 92, 118

Sackville, N.B. 100
Safdie, Moshe 109, 202
Saint Andrew's Anglican Cathedral, Victoria, B.C.
  83
Saint Andrew's Anglican Church, Lockport, Man.
  49
Saint Andrew's United Church, Moose Jaw, Sask.
  168
Saint Brigide, Montreal, Que. 86
Saint Dunstan's Roman Catholic Cathedral,
  Charlottetown, P.E.I. 76
Saint James-the-Less Chapel, Toronto, Ont. 81
Saint-Jean, Que. 18
Saint John the Baptist Roman Catholic Basilica,
  St. John's, Nfld. 86
Saint John's Anglican Church, Saint John, N.B. 47
St. John's, Nfld. 36, 86
Saint Mary's Anglican Church, Auburn, N.S. 26
Saint Mary's Church, Red Deer, Alta. 194
Saint Patrick's Roman Catholic Church,
  Medicine Hat, Alta. 73
Saint Paul's Angilcan Church, Dawson, Yukon 50
Saint Paul's Anglican Church, Trinity, Nfld. 57
Saint Paul's presbyterian Church, Hamilton, Ont.
  55
Saint Saviour's, Barkerville, B.C. 55
Saskatchewan 31, 96, 116, 121, 123, 130, 135,

138, 155, 168, 174, 192
Saskatchewan Hall, Saskatoon, Sask. 168
Saskatchewan Legislative Building, Regina, Sask.
  121
Saskatoon, Saskatchewan 96, 130, 168
Saxe, Charles C. 164
Schofield, John 96
School of Architecture, Carleton University,
  Ottawa, Ont. 187
Seminaire, Quebec City, Que. 20
Sharon, Maurice 155
Sheppard, H., and G. Masson 150
Simon Fraser University, South Bernaby, B.C. 196
Sise (of Affleck, Desbarats, Demakopoulos,
  Lebensold and Sise) 186
Smith Carter Architects 199
South Burnaby, B.C. 196
South Park Elementary School, Victoria, B.C. 105
Spence, Jerome 170
Sproatt, Henry, and Ernest Rolph 167
Stechesen Katz 199
Stinson, J. and C. Corneil 187
Storm, William 85
Storey, Edgar, and William Van Egmund 130, 138
Sullivan, Francis 172, 173, 175

Taché, E.E. 94
Taylor, A.T. 83
Theatre Montcalm, Quebec City, Que. 116
Thomas, William 55, 60
Thomson Building, Timmins, Ont. 150
Thompson, Berwick and Pratt 190
Thompson, N.L., and H. Hargreaves 174
Timmins, Ont. 150
Toronto City Hall, Toronto, Ont. 195
Toronto, Hamilton and Buffalo Railway Station,
  Hamilton, Ont. 149
Toronto-Dominion Centre, Toronto, Ont. 182
Toronto, Ont. 81, 85, 90, 107, 112, 121, 124,
  142, 146, 167, 179, 182, 195
Town Hall, Melville, Sask. 138
Townley and Matheson 134
Trapp Building, New Westminster, B.C. 125
Trinity, Nfld. 57
Tryon United Church, Tryon, P.E.I. 81
Tryon, P.E.I. 81

Union Bank Building, Winnipeg, Man. 125
Union Station, Toronto, Ont. 112
University College, University of Toronto,
 Toronto, Ont. 85
University of British Columbia, Vancouver, B.C.
 190
University of Regina, Regina, Sask. 192
University of Saskatchewan, Saskatoon, Sask. 168
University of Toronto, Toronto, Ont. 85, 167, 179
Upper Canada 13

Vallance (Brown and) 168
Van der Rohe, Mies 182
Van Egmund, William (Storey and) 130, 138
Vancouver, B.C. 96, 134, 140, 145, 156, 164,
 190, 203
Victoria and Grey Trust Building, Kingston, Ont.
 42
Victoria Rifles Armoury, Montreal, Que. 170
Victoria, B.C. 83, 100, 105

Wagner (Fellheimer and) 149
Warehouse, Fort St. James, B.C. 16
Watkins (Hooper and) 105
Watts, John W.H. 100
Watson, Sask. 116
Webb Zerafa 199
Weins, Clifford 192
Western Canada 15
Weyburn, Sask. 155
Wills, Frank 52
Wilson, W.R. 105
Windsor Station, Montreal, Que. 88
Winnipeg, Man. 92, 100, 118, 125, 128, 188, 199
Wolfville, N.S. 150
Woolford, J.E. 24

Yukon 50, 115

Zerafa (Webb Zerafa) 199

Printed in Canada